Sexy W... for Writers

by Stefanie Olsen

Published by

Choose-A-Sexy-Ending Erotic Books

Copyright 2013 Stefanie Olsen

Dear Reader

The editor and illustrator worked very hard to make this the best possible book.
If you enjoy it, please pay the very reasonable asking price.
Thank you for reading and respecting.

Table of Contents

NOTE from the Editor

Thank you for downloading the Spring 2013 version of **Words for Sexy Writers**, containing new entries- like *Said, Thought, and Naughty*- and links between relevant sections. We look forward to hearing your comments and suggestions for future updates! We're particularly interested in knowing if you found a word or concept lacking or absent while penning a sex scene.

As a resource for writers of romance and erotica, entries here lean toward the pleasant side of life- so under *Vocalizations* one will find fewer "whining rants" and more "lyrical whispers", accompanied by quite a few moans and screams.

To facilitate creative leaps of inspiration, entries are sorted by situation and character rather than parts of speech, so "attention", "beguile", and "magnetism" all appear under *Allure*. Many words show up in more than one category. Again, we hope to make your task easier by giving your overworked neurons fodder for new creative connections.

We've grouped some descriptors according to traditional gender roles for simplicity's sake, though we're perfectly aware that men can be fragile and women can be implacable. In this case the choice was based on anatomical allegory and intended audience. In sex scenes we often need our men to be big and hard and our women to be soft and pliant, if not in real life.

The first half of **Words for Sexy Writers** is organized chronologically by order of events:

Our main characters meet, get to know one another, develop an attraction, do interesting and exciting things to each other. The sex act is also organized chronologically, from *Undressing* through *Afterglow*.

The second half of the book is devoted to more general terms useful in sex scenes.

While we acknowledge the existence of hundreds of slang terms for various sexual acts and body parts, most of them belong in a different book. We limited ourselves to terms that could conceivably be used in mainstream novels without making the reader giggle or throw up. Please feel free to consult any of the online slang dictionaries for a fuller exploration of today's up-to-the-minute teenage terminology.

The same goes for exhaustive lexicons of historical time periods and individual fetish props, participants, and terminology. **Words for Sexy Writers** limits itself to a separate category at the end for slightly rougher terminology.

Thank you!

Stefanie Olsen, ed.

Once upon a time,

there was a beautiful princess living in the loftiest tower of a castle in a faraway land.

The princess spent hours gazing wistfully out the window, dreaming of the day a prince would come and free her family from the prison created by her evil stepfather. Instead, the vicious man banished her from her home, selling her into marriage with a sadistic villain in an untamed foreign land.

3

Meeting

Appearance, seemed, obviously

Absolutely, address, affectation, air, apparently, appear [to be], appearance, aspect, assume [appearance], at first blush, at first sight, attitude, aura, be visible, bearing, behavior, beyond any doubt, blush, by the skin of one's teeth, carriage, carried [oneself], cast, categorically, certainly, character, characteristics, clearly, comportment, condition, conduct, considerably, conspicuously, contours, countenance, course, cut [of one's clothing or sails], cut a figure, decidedly, definitely, deliberately, demeanor, demonstrated, deportment, display, distinctly, doubtlessly, dressed as though, especially, evidently, exhibit, explicitly, expression, expressly, face, far and away, features, fervently, figure, firmly, form, front, gave the impression, guise, impression, in the eyes of, incontestably, incontrovertibly, indicated, indisputably, indubitably, intentionally, intimately, it would seem, jointly, lines, looked like, manifest, manifestly, manner, mannerism, markedly, meticulously, mien, mindfully, mood, nearly, notably, noticeably, obviously, officially, on the face of it, openly, ostensibly, outwardly, particularly, patently, physiognomy, plain to see, plainly, pose, positively, posture, presence, presented [appearance], prima facie, professed [to be], profile, properties, quality, remarkably, resembled, scrupulously, seem to be, seemingly, semblance of, sharply, show [of], signally, spectacle, stamp, strictly, strike as, strikingly, surely, tableau, [the] image [of], thoughtfully, to a great extent, to all appearances, to the naked eye, took the shape of, traits, undeniably, undoubtedly, unequivocally, unmistakably, unquestionably, visage, visibly, without doubt, without question, wore [appearance]

See also Beautiful, Handsome

Allure, attract

Affect, affinity, allure, appeal, arouse, attention, attract, bait, beguile, bewitch, bid, cajole, captivate, charm, chemistry, coax, come-on, command, courting, demand, desirable, disturb, draw in, enchant, endear oneself, engage, enthrall, entice, entrap, excite, fascinate, feel out, follow, gesticulate, gesture, gravitate, guide, hook, impress, inducement, influence, inspire, interest, inveigle, invitation, invite, lead on, lure, magnetism, make an impression, mark, melt, motion to, move, nod, persuade, pursue, pull, quicken, rope in, seduce, seduction, sign, signal, spellbinding, steering, stimulate, stirring, striking, strike a chord, suck in, summon, sway, sweep off feet, tempt, temptation, tendency, thrill, tug at the heart, turn on, upset, wave, wiles, win over

See also Desirous

Look, see, watch

Admire, apprehend, ascertain, assess, attend, attention, attentive, be on alert, be on the lookout, be vigilant, be wary, be watchful, behold, care for, cast [an eye at], catch sight of, check out, concentrate [on], consider, contemplate, detected, devote oneself, differentiate, discern, discover, distinct, distinguished, divine, eagle-eye, espied, examine, eye, eyeball, feast [one's] eyes, focused on, follow [with one's eyes], gape, gawk, gaze, get a load of, [give one the] evil eye, give the once over, glance, glimpse, glower, goggle, guard, have a look-see, hearken, heed, inspect, introspection, keep [one's] eye on, keep eyes open, keep eyes peeled, keep tabs, keeping watch, lay [one's] eyes on, leer, look, look after, look out, look-see, made out, mark, mind, mind the store, note, noted, notice, observe, ogle, once-over, oversee, pay attention, pay heed, peek, peep, peer, perceive, pick out, pick up on, pore over, read, reconnaissance, regard, regarding, registered, remark, review, rubberneck, scan, scope, scout, scrutinize, see, see through, sight, slant, spotted, spy, squint, stare, study, superintend, supervise, surveillance, survey, [take a] gander, take heed, take in [the sight], take notice [of], tend, view, watch, watch over, witness

New, different

A distinct, a far cry from, a further, a separate, altered, anomaly, antithesis, at odds, at variance, atypical, bizarre, brand-new, change, clashing, contrary, contrast, current, cutting-edge, deviant, dewy, different, discrepancy, disparate, dissimilar, distant, distinct, distinctive, divergent, diverse, exceptional, farther, fashionable, flaky, fresh, further, incomparable, inconsistent, individual, inexperienced, irregular, latest, like night and day, mismatched, modern, modernistic, modish, more, new, newfangled, novel, odd, offbeat, one more, original, other, otherwise, particular, peculiar, poles apart, recent, single, some other, something else, state-of-the-art, strange, topical, ultramodern, unaccustomed, unequal, unfamiliar, unique, unknown, unlike, unnatural, unrelated, unusual, up-to-date, weird

Think, thought, plan

abstraction, afterthought, aim, analyze, anticipate, apply intellect, appraise, appreciate, apprehend, association of ideas, assume, attend, attention, aware, be advised, be uppermost in one's mind, bear in mind, beat one's brains, bethink oneself, big idea, big picture, brain wave, brainstorm, brood, bubble, cerebrate, cherish an idea, chew the cud, clue, cogitate, cogitation, cognition, collect one's thoughts, commune, comprehend, conceived, concentrate, concentration, concept, conceptualize, concerned, conclude, [stop to] consider, consideration, contemplate, cross [one's] mind, decide, deduce deliberation, delusion, derived, designs, digest, discern, dream/ daydream, engrossing, entertain [the notion], envision, estimate, evaluate, examine, exercise the intellect, factor, fancied, fantasize, feared, figure out, find, foresight, forethought, game plan, goal, grasp, hallucinate, harbor, have in mind, heed, hope, hypothesize, idea, illusion, image, imagine, impression, infer, inference, inkling, intellectualize, intend, intention, interpret, introspection, intuition, judge, ken, know, logic, machination, meaning, meditate, memory, mental picture, mind, mull [over], muse, new angle, nightmare, notion, nurture an idea, objective, occupy one's mind, occur, occurrence, opinion, penetrate, pensive, perceive, perplexing, philosophical, picture, pie in the sky, pipe dream, plan, play [with idea], plot, ponder, problem, projected, propose, proposition, purport, puzzle, rack/ ransack one's mind, rationalize, realize, reason, reconsider, reflect, regard, resolve, retrospection, reverie, review, ruminate, run over [in one's head/ mind], scenario, scheming, scope, scrutinize, see, sink in, slant, sleep on, sort out, specter, speculate, stew, strike, struck, studious, study, succession of ideas, suggest itself, suppose, take into account, take under consideration, theorize, theory, think, thoughtful, [train of/ lost in] thought, trance, turn over, turn over [in one's mind], under consideration, understand, use one's head, using one's wits, view, vision, weigh, wistful, wrinkle

See also Know, certain, genuine, Thoughtfully, Unconsciously, confused

He said, She said

See also Vocalizations, Hear, sound, audible, Promise, and Sounds (general)

Stated, agree

Acquaint, advise, allude to, apprise, aside, assent, assert, assume, assurance, attest, aver, avow, babble, back talk, bang, bark, bestow, blithe, blunt, bomb, boost, bouncy, breathe, bright, bring up, broach, bulletin, buoyant, burble, bury the hatchet, buzz, cackle, call, capitulate, casual remark, catchy, celebrate, certify, characterization, charge, chatter, cheerfulness, chime in, chipper, chirpy, choral, chronicle, cite, claim, close-mouthed, coax, come to terms, comeback, comfort, commend, comment, communicate, communiqué, compliment, concede, concession, concur, confess, confide, confidential, confirm, conjecture, connect [with], connotation, connote, consent, considered, console, contact, contract, converse, convey, cop a plea, cop-out, cordially, correspond, corroborate, counterclaim, courteously, cover up, crack, crash, creak, cry, cue, declaration, declare, deem, defend, defer to, define, delineate, delivered, depict, deposition, describe, description, details, dictum, directive, disarming, disclose, disclosure, discordant, dispassion, dispatch, disseminate, dissonant, divulge, drip, drone, drop, dulcet, dumb, ease up, echo, edict, effervescent, ejaculation, elucidate, emit, endorsed, endure, engaged, enlighten, enlivening, enthusiastic, enumerate, enunciate, equanimity, estimate, eulogize, excerpt, exclaim, excuse, explain, explication, expose, expository, express, extol, fable, facile, faintest idea, feedback, fiercely, fill in, fishing, fit in, foreshadow, gag, gay, genial, get across, get through, give an inkling, give blessing, go into details, gossip, grant, grapevine, greeting, growl, grunt, guarantee, gurgle, hail, harmonic, harmonious, harmony, hearsay, hearty, hint, hint [at], hiss, hold in, hopeful, hot, hum, hush, hushed, hypothetical, impart, implication, imply, impression, impugn, in accord/ chorus/

concert/ harmony/ step/ tune/ unison, inaudible, incongruous, indicate, indication, infer, inference, inflection, inform, infused, inject, innuendo, insert, inside story, insinuate, interact, interject, interpose, interpret, intimate, intimation, intone, introduce, intrude, inventory, jabber, jaunty, jocund, jolly, joyfully, justification, kindly, lap up, laud, leading, leak, let on, let up, letter, light, lilting, lively, low-down, lull, make nice, making public, meandering, meet halfway, mellifluous, melodic, melodious, mention, message, mitigate, moan, moderate, modulate, mollify, muffled, mumble, murmur, musical, mute, mutter, muzzle, narrate, narrative, neighborly, news, nice, nod, noiseless, noiselessness, nonchalant, not saying boo, noted, noticed, notified, oath, observe, offer, open up, operatic, oppose, optimistic, orchestral, own up, pacify, parting shot, pass on, patch things up, patter, pay dirt, peace, peaceful, peppy, perform, perky, picture, pitch, placate, placid, play on words, play the game, plea, plead, pleasing, point out, poise, polish, polite, portray, pour oil on, praise, prediction, press, pretext, proclaim, profess, prompt, pronouncement, prophecy, propose, publicize, publish, purr, put in, quell, quiet, quote, raise subject, ratify, rave, reaction, rebut, recall, recite, reckoned, recognized, recollection, recommend, record, recount, refer to, reflect, refute, rehearse, rein in, rejoinder, related, remark, remind, repartee, repetition, reply, report, represented, repressed, reserved, resolution, resolve, resonant, resonate, resounding, respectful, response, restrained, reticent, retort, return, reveal, revelation, reverberate, rhythmic, riposte, ripple, roar, root, rubber-stamp, rumor, run-down, said, salute, sanction, sanguine, satisfy, say, say in passing, saying, scandal, scoop, scuttlebutt, secretive, sedate, serene, shout, shriek, shrill, shush, sibilant, sigh, silent, silvery, simmered, sing, sketched, skinny, slack, slacken, slam, smash, smoothly, smother, snappy, snort, snugness, sobriety, sociably, soft-pedal, soften, solace, solicit, solution, song, sonorous, soothing, sound, soundless, speech, spiel, spill, spoke, spread rumor, squash, squawk, squeal, squeeze in, squelch, stage-whisper, stall, stammer, stamp of approval, stand for, state, statement, steady, story, stutter, submit, suggest, summarize, sunny, support, supposed, suppress, swallow, swear, sweeten, sweetly, sympathetic, symphonic, tale, talk, tally, tell, testimonial, testimony, thanks, tidings, tight-lipped, tip off, token, told, tone, tone down, tongue, toot, touch base, touch on, tranquil, translate, transmit, trickle, trumpet, tuneful, two cents' worth, uncover, undertone, unfold, upbeat, utter, utterance, vent, verbal, verbalize, verify, version, vibrate, vignette, vivacious, vocal, vocalization, vocalize, voice, vouch, warmth, whine, whir, whisper, wisecrack, word-of-mouth, yarn, yield, yield to, zingy, zippy

Loud, negative, disagreement

About-face, abstain, accusation, accuse, acerbic, acid, acrimonious, aggressive, allege, angry, annoyed, antagonistic, antagonize, argumentative, ascribe, assert, astringent, attack, austere, backpedal, backtrack, balk, bark, battling, bawl, bay, beef, begrudging, bellicose, belligerent, bellow, bellyache, bemoan, bewail, bicker, bitch, biting, bitter, blare, blaring, blasphemy, blowhard, blurt, bluster, boast, boisterous, bone of contention, booming, booming, brag, brawling, bray, broadcast, brush-off, brusque, bucking, burst out, cackle, cacophony, calamitous, call, canard, cantankerous, carp, caustic, caw, censorious, challenge, charge, chatter, churlish, clack, claim, clamor, clang, cluck, combative, comment, complain, conflict, confront, contention, contentious, contradict, contradiction, contradictory, contrary, crabby, cranky, crashing, criticize, cross, crotchety, crow, cruelly, cry, curse, cuss, cutting, dare, deafening, declaim, declare, defy, demand, demur, denial, denounce, deprecate, detectable, differ, difference, dire, disaffection;, disagree, disagreement, disapprove, disavow, disclaimer, discontent, discord, discordance, discouragement, discrepancy, dismiss, disown, disputed, dispute, dissension, dissent, distinct, dodge, doubt, earful, ejaculate, ejaculation, emit, emphatic, energetic, evade, exclamation, exhale, expletive, explode, expostulate, fabricate, falsehood, faultfinding, fierce, fight, find fault, forswear, fractious, fret, fretful, full, fuss, gainsay, gainsaying, gasp, give a hard time, gladiatorial, go on, gossip, grapevine, grieve, gripe, groan, grouchy, grouse, growl, grumble, grunt, guff, gush, harangue, harass, harsh, hassle, hateful, hearsay, heavy, hem and haw, heresy, heretic., hesitate, high-sounding, hiss, hold forth, holler, hoot, hostile, howl, hullabaloo, hurray, hurtful, ill-humored/ tempered, impatient, impetuous, indignant, innuendo, insinuate, insult, intemperate, intense, interject, interrogate, intrude, invent, irate, jarring, kick up a fuss, lament, lie, loud, loudmouthed, low, make a fuss, manifesto, mewling, moan, murmur, mutter, nag, negate, negative, nix, noisy, noncommittal, noncompliance, nonconformity, note, nullify, obnoxious, oppose, oratory, outcry, pant, peal, petulant, piercing, poignant, pontificate, proclaim, prohibit, protest, protest;, protestant, protestation, provoke, provoking, pussyfoot, put out, quack, quarrelsome, querulous, quick-tempered, ramble, rancorous, rant, raucous, rebuff, rebuke, rebuttal, recall, recant, refrain, refuse, refute, reject, rejection, remonstrate, rend, rending, renege, renounce, report, reprimand, reproach, repudiate, repudiation, repute, resist, resonate, resounding, retract, reverse, ringing, riotous, roar, rowdy, ruckus, rude, rumble, rumor, ruthless, sarcastic, sardonic, schism;, schismatic, scream, screech, scuttlebutt, sermonize, severe, sharp, shoot off one's mouth, short, shout, shriek, shrill, shy, snap, snarl, snivel, sob, sonorous, sound off, sour, spat, speech, spellbinding, splitting, squall, squawk, squeak, squeal, statement, stertorous, stinging, story, strident, strife, suggestion, sullen, summons, supposition, surly, taciturn, take exception to, tale, talk, tart, tattle, test, threaten, thunder, tidings, touchy, trill, truculent, trumpet, tumult, turn down, ugly, ultimatum, uncommunicative, ungracious, unpalatable, unrestrained, unruly, uproar, utter, vacillate, vehement, veto, vexatious, vindication, vitriolic, vociferation, vociferous, vulgar, vying, wail, waive, waking the dead, warning, waspish, waver, weep, wheeze, whimper, whine, whinny, whisper, whistle, whoop, wild, within earshot, woeful, word, wrathful, yammer, yap, yell, yelp, yip, yowl

Feelings

Affect, affection, agitation, anger, ardor, commotion, concern, desire, despair, despondency, disturbance, drive, ecstasy, elation, empathy, excitability, excitement, feeling, fervor, grief, gut reaction, happiness, inspiration, joy, love, melancholy, passion, perturbation, pride, rage, remorse, responsiveness, sadness, satisfaction, sensation, sensibility, sensitiveness, sentiment, shame, sorrow, sympathy, thrill, tremor, vehemence, vibes, warmth, zeal

See also Confused, Happily Ever After

Emotional, excited

Affectionate, anxious, ardent, building, bursting, candid, disturbed, ecstatic, effusive, emotional, emotive, enthusiastic, excitable, exciting, expansive, explanatory, explosive, expository, expressive, falling apart, fanatical, feeling, fervent, fervid, feverish, fickle, fiercely, fiery, frank, frenzied, glowing, gushing, heartwarming, heated, heightened, histrionic, hot-blooded, hysterical, impassioned, impetuous, impulsive, inflamed, intense, intoxicating, irrational, loving, moved, nervous, open, outgoing, outpouring, outspoken, overwrought, passionate, pathetic, penetrating, poignant, profuse, responsive, roused, sensitive, sentient, sentimental, sharp, spontaneous, stabbing, stirring, stormy, susceptible, symptomatic, temperamental, tempestuous, tender, touching, unconstrained, unreserved, unrestrained, unsettled, volcanic, warm, warmhearted, zealous

Desirous

Ache, acquisitive, agog, aim, ambitious, anticipation, antsy, anxious, appeal, appetite, ardent, aroused, avid, blazing, boiling with lust, breathless, burn, burning, champing at the bit, churning, clamor, coursing through, covet/ous, craving, cry out for, demand, desirous, desperate, dream of, dying to, eager, earnest, electric charge, enthusiastic, entreaty, excitement, expectant, fancy, fanned the flame, fantasy, feel a need, hoard, fervent, fervid, fierce, fiery, fighting the urge, gluttonous, greedy, hankering, have a passion for, have a yen for, have eyes for, heated, horny, hot, hot to trot, hunger, hungry, impassioned, impatient, incline toward, insistence, intense, intent, interest, itch, keen, longing, lust, lusting after, panting after, partial to, passion, passionate, petition, pine, pining, predatory, prefer, propensity, pursuit, rapacious, rarin' to go, ravenous, ready and willing, restive, restless, salacious, selfish, squirming, thirsty, tingling, too close, torturous, urge, urgent, voracious, want, warm-blooded, wild, wish, yearning, yen, zealous

See also Allure

Love

Admire, adore, appreciate, affection, affections, amoré, animation, ardor, attachment, care, closeness, concern, craving, craze, crush, dedication, desire, devotion, drive, eagerness, ecstasy, emotion, endearment, enthusiasm, esteem, exaltation, excitement, fancy, fascination, feelings, fervor, fire, frenzy, friendliness, glorification, good will, hankering, heart, heat, honor, idol, idolatry, idolization, inclination, infatuation, intensity, ire, jazz, joy, kindness, liking, love, mania, misery, obsession, outbreak, outburst, paroxysm, passion, predilection, propensity, puppy love, rapture, regard, reverence, sentiment, soft spot, solicitude, spirit, sympathies, take a shine to, tenderness, veneration, warmth, weakness for, worship, yen, zeal, zest

As the princess' ship bucked across the dark ocean in a frightening storm, pirates cast an unseen line to board, absconding with the vessel's treasures. The most valuable cargo, the princess herself, was taken captive by the pirates' huge and menacing captain, legendary for both his skills and formidable temper.

Arousal

Lip service

Absorb, appreciate, attack, banquet, bite, bolt, breakfast, brush, champ, chaw, chew, chomp, chow down, clamp, consume, cram, crunch, crush, cunnilingus, darting, delve, devour, diet, digest, dine, dispatch, dispose of, down, eat, eat up, exist on, fall to, fare, feast, feast upon, feed, fellatio, gnaw, gobble, gorge, gourmet, graze, grind teeth, gulp, gum, guzzle, have a bite, hover, ingest, inhale, lap up, lash, lave, lick, lip, live on, lunch on, make a meal of, masticate, meal, morsel, mow, munch, murmur against, nibble, nip, nosh, nourish, nurture, nutrition, partake, peck, pick, pig out, pinch, pinch between lips, polish off, prey on, put away, put down, revel in, scarf, scoff up, seize, slurping, slice across, snack, snap onto, spend, stuff, stuff one's face, suck, suckle, suction, sup, swallow, swill, swirling, take a chunk out of, take in, taste, teethe, tongue, toss down, voracious, wolf, wound

See also Taste

Touch

Abrade, blow, brushing, butterfly, caress, circling, coax, concentrate on, contact, crushing, cupped, dancing, delve, digging in, dragging, embrace, explore, feel, fingering, flick, flicking, fluttering, fondle, glancing, graze, guide, hug, indulge, invading, kiss, kneading, locate, maneuver, manipulated, manipulation, mark, massage, masturbated, mauling, ministrations, molded it, molesting, pamper, pat, pay attention to, petting, pinching, pinning, please, plucking, plumping, poke, preparing, press against, pressing, probe, probing, questing, raking over, roam, rooting, rotating, rouse, rubbing, running over, scrape, seeking, skim, smashing, smooth, sought, spinning, stimulate, stimulating, stretching, strip, stroke, sweep, tapped, tickle, touch, toying with, traced, tugged, tweaking, twist

See also During

Wander

Circle, cover, cross, cruise, drift, encompass, explore, float, follow, make circuit, meander, pass over, play over, ply, prowl, ramble, range, reach, reconnoiter, roaming, rove, scour, search, spread, straggle, stray, stroll, sweep, trailed over, traipse, tramp, travel, traverse, trek

The Evil Adverb

See also He is…, She is…, Rough (manners, sound, & sensation)

Anxious, doubt

Afraid, aghast, agitated, alarmed, anguished, antsy, anxious, apprehensive, awkward, basket case, biting [one's] nails, bothered, bugging out, butterflies, cautious, choking, concerned, constrained, cynical, discomposed, dismayed, disquieted, distressed, disturbed, doubted, doubtful, doubting, dreading, dubious, edgy/ on edge, exercised, fearful, fidgety, foreboding, fretful, frozen, have cold feet, have a funny feeling, hung up [on], hyper, ill at ease, impatient, in a cold sweat/ dither/ tizzy, insecure, jittery, jumpy, leery, mistrustful, nervous, overwrought, perturbed, restive, restless, scared, shaken, shaky, shook up, skeptical, spooked, strained, strung out, suspicious, sweating bullets, tense, tied up in knots, tormented, troubled, tumult, turmoil, uncertain, uneasy, unglued, unsettled, upset, uptight, vexed, wary, watchful, wired, worried [sick], wreck, wrung out

Ardent, passionate, intense, thoroughly

Acutely, admiringly, affectionately, angrily, appreciatively, ardently, attentively, boldly, completely, dearly, devoted, distressingly, dotingly, earnestly, emotionally, endearingly, enraptured, ferociously, fervently, fervidly, fiercely, fondly, forcefully, frantically, furiously, genuinely, gravely, impassioned, intensely, irresistibly, kindly, longingly, lovingly, loyally, lustfully, madly, mightily, monstrous, movingly, no holds barred, passionately, profoundly, rapturously, respectfully, reverently, riotously, roughly, sadly, savagely, seriously, severely, stormily, surely, tempestuously, tenderly, terribly, thoroughly, turbulently, uncontrollably, vehemently, viciously, violently, wildly, yearningly, zealously

Calm, unworried, insensitive

Aloof, amiable, amicable, apathetic, been around twice, blah, blind, blind to, blithe, bored, callous, carefree, careless, civil, cold-blooded, collected, cool, cool as cucumber, cool-headed, could care less, couldn't care less, cruel, deaf, deaf to, detached, disenchanted, disentranced, disinterested, dispassionate, distant, don't give a damn, done it all, draggy, easy, emotionless, equable, feckless, flat, forgetful, gentle, glutted, hard, hard-bitten, hard-boiled, hard-hearted, hardened, hardhearted, heartless, heedless, impassive, impenitent, imperturbable, inattentive, incurious, indifferent, indurated, inflexible, inscrutable, insensate, insensible, insensitive, insentient, insouciant, inured, jaded, kind, knowing, lackadaisical, laid-back, languid, levelheaded, listless, lukewarm, mellow, moderate, moony, mundane, negligent, neutral, nonchalant, obdurate, oblivious, offhand, passive, patient, phlegmatic, placid, pleased, poised, relaxed, reserved, restful, satiated, satisfied, sedate, self-centered, self-possessed, serene, sick of, sophisticate, sophisticated, soulless, spiritless, stiff, still, stoic, stolid, stony, stubborn, supine, surfeited, temperate, thick-skinned, torpid, tough, toughened, unaffected, unbending, unbothered, uncaring, uncompassionate, unconcerned, undisturbed, unemotional, unexcitable, unexcited, unfeeling, unflappable, unimpressed, unimpressionable, uninterested, uninvolved, unmoved, unperturbed, unresponsive, unruffled, unsusceptible, unsympathetic, untouched, untroubled, unworried, weary, what the hell, wimpy, world-weary, worldly

Expanding, swollen

Adding, aggrandize, amplified, amplifying, animate, ascension, augmented, beefy, big, blimp, bloated, blooming, blossoming, blow up, bolster, broaden, budding, bulging, bulk up, bull, burgeoning, burly, corpulent, develop, developing, dilating, distend, distended, elephantine, engorged, enlarge, enlarged, erect, expanding, extended, exuberant, fan out, fatten, filling out, fleshy, flourishing, gargantuan, grow, growing, heaving, hefty, heighten, increasing, inflamed, inflate, large, lengthen, living, lush, luxuriant, magnified, maturing, meaty, mounting, multiply, mushrooming, open, ostentatious, overblown, oversize, pad, plump, ponderous, prolong, prosperous, protract, pudgy, puffed, puffy, pumped up, pyramid, rippling, rising, robust, showy, solid, spreading, sprouting, stout, stretching, swelling, swollen, thicken, thriving, totaling, tumescent, turgid, unfold, unfurl, up, upheaval, upsurge, vigorous, weighty, widening

Light, lightly

Agile, airy, breezy, carelessly, casually, daintily, delicately, easily, effortlessly, ethereal, faintly, flippantly, freely, gently, gingerly, mildly, moderately, nimbly, peacefully, quietly, readily, simply, slightly, smoothly, softly, sparingly, sparse, subtly, tenderly, tenuously, thinly, timid, unsubstantial

See also Sexy Clothing Words

Know, certain, genuine

Absolutely, accurately, actually, apparently, ascertain, assured, assuredly, authentically, beyond doubt/ question, categorically, certain, certainly, cinch, clear-cut, clearly, clinched, come hell or high water, conclusively, confirmed, confirmedly, constantly, content, correctly, de facto, decide, decided, decidedly, decisively, definite, definitely, dependable, determine, devotedly, doubtless, doubtlessly, easily, ensured, exactly, existing, factually, faithful, faithfully, firmly, fixed, for sure, genuinely, guaranteed, honestly, honorably, in actuality, in effect, in fact, in reality, in the bag, in truth, indisputably, indubitable, insured, irrefutable, legitimately, loyally, made certain, most likely, nailed down, no ifs ands or buts, no strings attached, of course, on ice, on the button, on the money, on the nose, ostensibly, positively, precisely, presumably, probably, pronounced, racked, real, really, reliably, right on, righteously, rightly, sealed, secure, seemingly, set, settled, sewed up, sincerely, staunchly, steadily, straight out, supposedly, sure, sure as can be, sure as hell, sure enough, sure thing, surefire, surely, tangible, the very thing, truly, trustful, truthfully, unambiguously, unconditionally, undoubted, undoubtedly, unequivocally, unquestionable, unquestionably, unsuspecting, unworried, veraciously, veritably, very, with all one's heart, with devotion, without a doubt, without doubt

Naughty

Aberrant, amoral, bad, badly behaved, base, bawdy, beguiling, blue, breezy, coarse, contrary, crafty, crooked, crude, cunning, daring, deceitful, deceiving, defiant, deviant, devil-may-care, devilish, devious, dirty, disobedient, earthy, erotic, erratic, explicit, fallible, fast, fiendish, filthy, forward, foul, foul-mouthed, free and easy, fresh, frolicsome, gross, hard-core, heretic, hot, ill-behaved, immodest, immoral, improper, impure, in bad taste, incontinent, indecent, indecorous, indelicate, indiscreet, juicy, knavish, lascivious, lecherous, lewd, libertine, libidinous, licentious, loose, lurid, lustful, misbehave, mischievous, miscreant, naughty, obscene, off-base, off-color, offending, offensive, out-of-line, perverse, pornographic, profligate, provocative, purple, questionable, racy, rakish, rascally, raunchy, raw, rebellious, ribald, riotous, risqué, rogue, rough, roving, rowdy, rude, salacious, salty, saucy, scandalous, shady, shameless, sinful, sizzling, slick, smart, smutty, spicy, stray, suggestive, taboo, teasing, treacherous, unbecoming, unchaste, unclean, unconventional, undisciplined, ungodly, unorthodox, unrefined, unrighteous, unruly, unseemly, untoward, vile, vulgar, wanton, wayward, wicked, willful, wrong, x-rated

See also Shocking, Evil

Quickly, easily

Abrupt, apace, bluff, blunt, boiled down, briskly, brusque, chop-chop, competently, concise, crisp, curt, dexterously, efficiently, effortlessly, ephemeral, evenly, expeditiously, fast, flat-out, fleeting, fleetly, full tilt, handily, hastily, hasty, hurriedly, immediately, in a flash, in haste, in nothing flat, in short order, instant, instantaneously, instantly, laconic, lickety-split, lightly, like a bat out of hell, like a flash, like a shot, like greased lightning, like wildfire, limited, little, passing, pithy, posthaste, presto, promptly, pronto, quick, quickly, rapidly, readily, sharp, short and sweet, skimpy, small, smoothly, snippy, soon, speedily, steadily, succinct, surely, surly, swift, swiftly, terse, to the point, well

See also Skillful, Experienced

Slow, sleepy, relaxed

Absent, abstracted, all in, apathetic, asleep, assuage, at ease, balm, beat, becalm, bedraggled, burned out, bushed, calm, catnap, collapsed, coma, comatose, comfortable, compose, conk [out], crash, dead, debilitated, disengaged, dopey, dormant, downtime, doze, dragging, drained, dream, drooping, drop off, dropping, drowse, drowsy, dull, ease, easy, empty, enervated, enfeebled, exhausted, fading, fagged, faint, failing, fall asleep, fatigue, fatigued, feeble, flagging, flop, forty winks, halt, heavy, heedless, hibernate, [hit the] rack, holiday, hush, idle, immobile, inactive, inattentive, incapacitated, inert, interlude, intermission, interval, lackadaisical, lagging, laid-back, languid, languish, languor, languorous, lassitude, lax, lay back, laze [about], lazy, leaden, lean, leisurely, lethargic, lethargy, letup, lifeless, limp, listless, loaf, loll, lounge, low-key, lull, moon[about], mope, motionless, motionlessness, nap, nod [off], out of [gas/ it], pacify, paralyzed, passive, peaceful, phlegmatic, played out, pooped, powerless, prone, prostrate, put [one's] feet up, quiescent, quiet, recess, recline, recumbent, refresh, relax, relief, relieved, repose, respite, rest, retire, run-down, rusty, sack out, sapped, sated, satiated, sawing wood, sedate, sedentary, settle, shut-eye, siesta, silent, slack, slake, sleep, sleepy, slothful, slow, sluggard, sluggish, slumber, slumped, snooze, snore, somnolent, soothe, spent, sprawl, stable, standstill, steady, still, stretch out, stupor, supine, [take a] breather, take five/ ten, tired, torpid, torpor, tranquil, tuckered [out], turn in, unhurried, unresponsive, unwind, vacant, washed out, wasted, weakened, weary, winding down, worn-out, yawning, zonked [out], zzz

See also Recline

Thoughtfully, watchfully

Alert, all eyes, attentive, carefully, cautious, chary, circumspect, consciously, deliberate, determinedly, discreetly, earnestly, exacting, fervently, grave, guarded, heedful, intentionally, intently, intimately, keen, meticulously, mindfully, minutely, observant, on guard, open-eyed, passionately, prepared, prudently, punctiliously, purposefully, ready, resolutely, scrupulously, searchingly, sincerely, soberly, solemnly, suspicious, thoughtfully, vigilant, vigorous, wary, wide-awake, zealously

Unconsciously, confused

Absent-minded, absorbed, abstract, ad-lib, addled, air-headed, at a loss, at sea, at sixes and sevens, automatically, baffled, befuddled, bemused, bewildered, carelessly, catching flies, caught off balance, coming apart, confounded, daydreaming, dazed, delirious, discombobulated, disconcerted, disoriented, disregarding, distracted, disturbed, divert, dreamy, engrossed, entertaining [other thoughts], extemporaneously, faraway, fazed, flummoxed, flustered, forgetful, out of habit, head in the clouds, heedless, impromptu, impulsive, inattentive, irrational, lead astray, lightheaded, lost [in thought], mixed up, moony, muddled, neglectfully, nonplussed, not with it, oblivious, occupied [by other], off balance, out of it, out to lunch, perplexed, perturbed, preoccupied, punch-drunk, punchy, puzzled, rattled, remote, removed, ruffled, scatterbrained, shaken up, sidetracked, spacey, spontaneously, stumped, unaware of surroundings, taken aback, thoughtlessly, thrown [off balance], torment, troubled, unaware of [events], unbalanced, unconsciously, unglued, unheeding, unhinged, unintentionally, unknowingly, unmindful, unsettled, unthinkingly, unwittingly, upset, mind wandering, thoughts elsewhere, withdrawn, without thinking, wool-gathering

Wet, liquid

Aqueous, awash, baptize, bathe, bead, bit, bleed, bubble, cascade, clammy, coating, crème, creamy, dab, damp, dank, dash, deluge, dew/ drop, dewy, diffuse, dip, discharge, distill, douse, drain, drench, drenched, dribble, driblet, drip, drizzle, drizzling, drop, droplet, drown, dunk, eddy, ejaculate, eject, emanate, erupt, excrete, expel, exude, flooding, flow, foggy, get in a lather, get wet, give, glistening, glow, gush, honey, hose, humidify, immerse, iota, irrigate, jet, juices, lather, lave, leak, leak out, let off, lubrication, mist, misty, moist, moisten, molecule, morsel, muggy, nip, off, oiled-up, ooze, ounce, overflow, particle, pearl, percolate, permeate, perspire, pinch, plop, plunge, pooled, potion, pour, precipitate, puddle, rain, rainy, rinse, ripple, run over, saturate, secrete, secretions, seep, seethe, semen, sheen of moisture, shower, showery, sip, slick, slimy, slippery, smidgen, soak, sodden, soggy, sop, sopping, soused, speck, spew, spill, spit, splash, spot, spray, sprinkle, squirt, steaming, steep, stormy, stream, submerge, submerse, swelter, taste, tear, teardrop, teem, tide, trace, trickle, trill, wash, water, weep, weeping, well, wet

Forced by cruel fate to endure hours in the company of the barbarous pirate, the princess' alarm turned to indignation and her sharp tongue pierced his formerly impregnable armor of composure. Prodded beyond endurance, the pirate tossed the disrespectful wench over his knee and paddled her, hurting his pride more than her bottom.

25

Sensations

Burn, tingle, ache

Ache, affliction, aggrieve, agonize, agony, ail, amuse, anguish, annoyance, awareness, beat, bite, blare, blaze, blush, brighten, brush, burning, caress, catch, chafe, consciousness, creeping, crick, cut to the quick, delight, discomfort, disquiet, distress, dull, excitement, excruciating, feeling, feverish, filled with, flame, flare, flush, flutter, gleam, glimmer, glitter, grip, gut reaction, have goose bumps, hurt, ignite, inflamed, injury, irk, irritation, itch, kindle, kink, malady, misery, pang, nick, pain, painful, palpitation, pang, paroxysm, perception, pet, pinch, please, pounding, pressure, prick, prickle, pulsate, pulse, punish, racked with, radiate, redden, resonate, response, rile, rose, rouge, sadden, sense, sensibility, sensitiveness, sensitivity, sentiment, sharp, shine, shiver, sickness, smart, smarting, smolder, snapping, snip, soreness, spasm, squeeze, stabbing, stimulate, sting, stitch, strain, stress, stretch, suffer, suffused with, susceptible, tension, thrill, throbbing, throes, thump, tickle, tingle, titillate, torment, torture, touch, tremble, tweak, twinge, twinkle, twitching, twitter, upset, vibes, vibration, worry, wound

See also Touch, Wander, Hands

Hearing, listen, audible

Apparent, appreciable, apprehend, ascertain, attend, audible, aural, check, clear, concentrate [on], conspicuous, crisp, deafening, decided, definite, definitive, detect, detectable, discernible, distinct, distinguishable, eavesdrop, evident, fixed, full, hear, hearken, heed, incisive, lend an ear, listen, make out, manifest, marked, minute, note, notable, noticeable, obvious, overhear, patent, pay heed, perceivable, perceptible, pick up, plain, prescribed, pronounced, recognizable, resounding, sensible, strain, take in, tangible, unambiguous, understandable, unequivocal, unmistakable, verify, well-defined

Sound (general)

Aural, babble, bang, blare, boom, breathe, buffeting, burble, burst, buzz, chime, chink, clamor, clang, clap, clatter, clear, clink, crack, crash, croon, deafening, detonate, din, ding, drip, droning, drum, echo, exhalation, explosion, fizz, fizzle, flapping, flowing, flutter, gasp, growl, gurgle, hint, hiss, honk, huff, hum, hushed, jangle, loud, moan, mumble, murmur, mutter, noise, peal, plink, purr, rasp, rattle, report, resounding, reverberate, ring, ringing, ripple, roaring, ruffle, rumble, rush, rustle, scream, sibilant, sigh, slam, smash, sound, stage-whisper, stammer, stutter, swell, tap, throb, thrum, thump, thunder, ting, tingle, tinkle, toot, trickle, trill, trumpet, undertone, voice, waft, wail, warble, wave, wham, whir, whirl, whisper, whistle, within earshot, zoom

Smell, taste

Adorable, ambrosial, appealing, appetizing, aromatic, balmy, choice, comestible, culinary, dainty, darling, delectable, delicious, delightful, diffuse, disperse, digestible, distinctive, divine, edible, enjoyable, enticing, evocative, exquisite, fit, flavorsome, fragrant, fruity, good, gratifying, heavenly, inviting, like candy, luscious, lush, mellow, mouthwatering, nice, nutritious, nutritive, odoriferous, odorous, palatable, perfumed, permeated, pervade, piquant, pleasant, pungent, rare, redolent, reminiscent, rich, safe, salty, satisfying, savory, scented, scintillating, scrumptious, sour, spicy, succulent, sugar-coated, sugary, sweet, sweet-scented, sweet-smelling, sweetened, tantalizing, tasteful, tasty, tempting, titillating, toothsome, well-prepared, well-seasoned, wholesome, yummy

See also Lip Service, Mouth

Undressing

Air, array, bare, blazon, brandish, cast off, demonstrate, demonstration, disclose, discover, display, disrobe, disrobed, divest, divulge, doff, emerge, exhibit, expose, flash, flaunt, flourish, guise, impression, indicate, lay bare, lay out, lose, manifest, materialize, mount, offer, parade, pare, peel, present, presentation, proffer, prove, pull off, remove, reveal, revealed, rip off, set out, shed, show, show off, showcase, showing, shuck, skin, slip/ slide out of, sport, spread, spread-eagle, streak, strip, take it off, unbutton, unclothe, uncover, undress, unfasten, unfold, unfurl, untie, unveil, vaunt, view, unraveling, tattering, threw off, dismantle, denuded, shredded, discarded, tore, wrested, nude, naked, unwrap, ripped

A few sexy clothing words

Belt, bewitching, bodice, briefs, bustier, corset, cups, delicate, diaphanous, displayed, encased in, ethereal, exposed, exquisite, filmy, fine, fine-drawn, fine-grained, fine-spun, flimsy, flowing, form-fitting, fragile, garter, gauzy, glistening, gossamer, impalpable, lace, light, lightweight, little, loose, lustrous, mask, minute, off-the-shoulder, panties, porous, powdery, pushed up, quality, revealing, ribbon, ripped, scanty, see-through, sheer, silk, silken, silky, skimpy, skirt, sleek, slippery, slender, slick, small, smooth, soapy, stockings, thin, thong, threadlike, ties, tore, translucent, transparent, veil, velvet, velvety, visible, waistband, wet

A few sexy supporting roles

Bedpost, canopy, pillows, bed, cushions, chair, ottoman, chaise, bench, table, desk, seated, swing, staircase, plush carpet, settee, couch, divan, sheer curtains, chamber, tower, fireside, hearth, swing, hayloft, shower, château, citadel, fortress, hold, keep, manor, mansion, palace, stronghold, villa , bolster, dwelling, estate, great hall, hamlet, village, shelter, niche, nook, perch

Thankful only that her humiliation took place in the privacy of the captain's cabin, the princess was appalled to find herself fantasizing about the pirate's warm lap and the flexing muscles of his thighs beneath her belly. Flustered by her growing awareness of him as a man and determined to avoid another spanking, she curbed her insolent nature.

e, hesitant, ound, mi imb, dizzy
s eyes, climax, peak, point, merciless. contract,
e, mouth, coax, grabbed her thigh. conclude. com
oting, risk, rotated, dark, rubbing, closed, his finger
ked in, move, confine, lustrous, control, massag
addling him, ruthlessly, straining, savagely,
upling, determined, seat, convince, corner, moving
e, impel, widespread, delve, demand, sink, alive, deny, desire, avid, ardor, dive

Doing It

See also Physical Position, Body Parts & Descriptions

During

Accept, allow access, arranging, astride, attain, awaited, back and forth, bent over, bounced, bowing, breach, breathlessly, bucked, buildup, cadence, clamping, clasped, claw, closer and closer, clung, complete, constricted, cushioning, deeper, defenseless, deliberate, digging, dipped, directed, driving, encouraging, engulfing, erotic, exposed, filled, flow, frantically, full, fullness, grew accustomed to, grimacing, grind, gripping, guided into, hidden, hold, hot, humping, in and out, insistent, instinctively, intrusion, invasion, inward, jerked, jiggled, jiggling, jostled, jounce, measure, melted, moved, pitched, presenting, pressing, pulse, pumping, reciprocal, regularity, replaced, responsive, return, rhyme, rhythm, rise and fall, rocking, rolled, rooting, rotated, rubbing, rushed, ruthlessly, savagely, sawing, scratch, secret, seed, sensuously, sexy, shielded, sinuous, slamming, sliding, slowing, smeared, splayed, spread, squeeze, squirming, staccato, straddling, straining, stretching, successive, succulent, surrender, sway, swing, tempo, tense, thrashing, tighten, tumbling, twisting, unable, undulated, unexpected, unleash, vibrations, wave, wider, wiggling, willing, worked up, writhing

Insert, fill

Admit, barge in, bayonet, bore, break in, burrow, burst in, bury, charge forward, cram, deeper, descend, deposit, dig in, drag in, drill, driving, drop in, embark, embed, enclose, encroach, enfold, enter, establish, entrenched, fall into, fill, find a way in, fixate, force, forge, gain entrée, gather, get inside, go in, go through, hammer in, horn in, imbed, impact, impale, implant, infiltrate, infuse, ingress, inject, inlay, insert, insinuate, install, instill, interlope, introduce, intrude, invade, jab, jam-pack, knife, load, lodge, make way, mount, move in, nail, occupy, peg, penetrate, perforate, pierce, pile in, plant, plunge, pop in, pounce, press, prick, probe, prod, puncture, push, put in, ram, ream, root, rush in, seat, set, settle, shoehorn, shove in, sink into, situate, slip, spear, squeeze in, stab, stick into, stuff in, swaddle, take up space, tamp, thrust in, top off, trespass, tuck, wedged, wend, work in, worm in, wriggled

See also Yield, Push Into

Lovemaking

Action, be carnal, "be with", bed, birds and the bees, boning, breed, bumping uglies, canoodling, caress, caressing, carnal knowledge, cohabit, coitus, conjugate, copulation, coquetting, couple, coupling, courting, cuddling, dalliance, do it, doing the dirty, doing the wild thing, embracing, facts of life, fondling, fool around, fooling around, foreplay, fornicate, fornication, generation, get laid, getting some, go all the way, go to bed, have relations, heavy petting, hook up, hugging, intercourse, intimacy, kissing, lay, lie with, lovemaking, magnetism, make it, make love, make out, making love, making out, mate, mating, nailing, necking, nookie, nooky, oral sex, parking, petting, plugging, poontang, procreation, relations, reproduction, roll in the hay, screwing, screwing around, sensuality, sex, shagging, sleeping together, sleeping around, smooching, snuggling, sucking face, tapping, unite

See Ruined/ Despoiled for lovemaking with loss of virginity

Orgasm, ejaculation

Abandon, achieve, alleviate, attain, big o, bolt of lighting, burst in pleasure, bust a nut, climax, conclude, crescendo, crest, cum, cumming, ecstasy, end, explode, feel the earth move, finish, fireworks, fulfill, furor, get off, glory, loss of control, orgasm, over the edge, paroxysm, peak, pearl necklace, pinnacle, rapture, reach the heights, release, relief, satisfaction, seeing god, spilling seed, spurting, succeed, summit, the little death, throes of passion, top, ultimate, uncoiled, unload, zenith

See also Bliss, Pleasure

Push into

Accelerate, advance, assault, attack, bang, bash into, batter, bear down, beat, blow, budge, buffet, bulldoze, bump, butt against, charge, coerce, collide, crowd, dig, drive, driving, energy, exertion, flail, flog, force, forcing, glance, goad, hammer, impact, impel, incite, influence, inspire, jab, jam, jolly [along], jolt, jostle, kid, knock, launch/ lurch into, lean, lean/ lie on, mass, move, muscle, nail, nudge, onset, pat, pellet, pelt, percuss, persuade, plow, poke, pound, pour it on, press, press with force, pressure, prod, propel, punch, push forward, railroad, ram, rammed, rap, ream, rest on, shift, shock, shoulder, shove, shoving, slammed, slap, slide into, smack, spank, speed, spur, squash, squeeze, squish, steamroll, straining, strike, stroke, strong-arm, swat, sway, tap, thrash, thump, turn [it] on, urge, wallop

See also Withdraw, Insert

Repeat

Amplify, augment, continue, do again, drive home, drum into, duplicate, dwell on, echo, endeavor, endure, enlarge, follow through/ up, follow up, go on, go over again, go the limit, grind away, hammer home, hold on, imitate, impress upon, increase, keep on, keep up, last, linger on, loop, magnify, multiply, obtain, peg away, persevere, persist, plug away, pound away, prevail, pursue, reciprocate, recur, redo, redouble, renew, reoccur, repeat, replicate, reprise, reproduce, return, revert, see through, stick it out, stick to, strive, stubborn, supplement, tough it out

See also Forever

Shaking

Clenching, clutched, clutching, contractions, convulsions, flinch, flutter, jolt, pulsations, pulsed, quake, quaking, quiver, quivering, shaking, shivers, shivering, shudder, spasms, trembled, tremors

See also Orgasm, ejaculation

Vocalizations

Acknowledge, affirm, announce, appeal, argue, arouse, ask, avow, awaken, babble, bark, bawl, bay, begging, bellow, bemoan, beseech, bewail, blending, blubber, boisterous, break down, burble, burst into tears, buzz, cajole, caterwaul, chimed, choke up, choked, claim, clamor, clamorous, coax, comeback, complain, contend, cried out, croaking, croaky, croon, cry, cry out, cursing, cussing, declare, deep, defend, deny, disprove, dispute, dissolve in tears, drone, dulcet, echo, entreat/y, exclaim, exclamation, explain, fret, gasped, gnarl, grieve, groan, groaned, growl, gruff, grumble, grunt, gulped, gurgle, guttural, hail, harmonious, harsh, hissed, hoarse, holler, hoot, howl, hum, hushing, huskily, husky, implore, importune, insistent, keen, keening, lament, let go, let it all out, lilting, loud, low, lyrical, maintain, make a fuss, mellow, melodic, mewl, moan, moaned in pleasure, mourn, mumble, murmur, musical, mutter, noisy, object, obscenities, offer, outcry, panting, parry, peeped, petition, plaint, plead, praise, pray, proclaim, profess, proposed, protest, purr, ragged sobs, rasping, raucous, recount, refute, rejoinder, remark, resolve, respond, retaliate, rhythmic, ripple, roar, roll, rough, rouse, rumble, rustle, sass, scold, scratchy, scream, screech, shout, shriek, shushing, sigh, silvery, sing, snarl, sniff, sob, sonorous, sound, squealed, squelch, stammer, state, strum, stutter, swearing, sweet, sweet-sounding, testify, throatily, throaty, throb, thrum, thunder, trill, tuneful, urging, vehement, vibrate, vocal, wail, waken, warble, weep, wheeze, whimper, whine, whinny, whisper, whoop, wish, yell, yelp, yip, yowl

See also Said, Sound (general), Hearing

The pirate couldn't believe such a
fragile and feminine lady caused the furor in his veins,
nor that he'd allowed himself to lose control. Chagrined,
he tried to be kinder, thinking the delicate princess was
likely terrified by her predicament and her audacious
demeanor merely false and bewitching bravado.

Afterglow

Pull, withdraw

Abandon, cast loose, cease, clear away, detach, disengage, dislodge, displace, disturb, drag, draw toward, evacuate, expel, extract, extricate, free, gather, get rid of, haul, heave, issue, jerk, let go of, liberate, loose, loosen, lug, obstruct, oust, pick, pluck, pry, pull out, relinquish, release, remove, rend, rip, rip out, separate, set free, set loose, strain, stretch, surrender, take out, tear, tear out, tow, tug, twitch, unseat, uproot, wrench, wrest, yank

Snuggle

Be true to, bear hug, blanket, buss, care for, cherish, clasp, cleave to, clinch, cling to, cloak, clutch, coddle, cohere, comfort, conceal, continue, coop, corral, cosset, cover, cradle, cuddle, cultivate, dandle, dote on, drape, embrace, encircle, enclose, encompass, encourage, enfold, engulf, enshrine, enshroud, entwine, envelop, feel, fence, fold, fondle, foster, guard, handle, hang in, harbor, hold dear, hold fast, honor, hug, idolize, kiss, last, like, linger, lock, love, make love, massage, mug, neck, nestle, nourish, nurse, nurture, nuzzle, pat, pet, play around, prize, protect, revere, roll, rub, safeguard, shelter, shield, snuggle, squeeze, stay put, stroke, surround, sustain, swaddle, swathe, take in arms, touch lovingly, treasure, value, venerate, worship, wrap in arms

Slow, sleepy, relaxed

Absent, abstracted, all in, apathetic, asleep, assuage, at ease, balm, beat, becalm, bedraggled, burned out, bushed, calm, catnap, collapsed, coma, comatose, comfortable, compose, conk [out], crash, dead, debilitated, disengaged, dopey, dormant, downtime, doze, dragging, drained, dream, drooping, drop off, dropping, drowse, drowsy, dull, ease, easy, empty, enervated, enfeebled, exhausted, fading, fagged, faint, failing, fall asleep, fatigue, fatigued, feeble, flagging, flop, forty winks, halt, heavy, heedless, hibernate, [hit the] rack, holiday, hush, idle, immobile, inactive, inattentive, incapacitated, inert, interlude, intermission, interval, lackadaisical, lagging, laid-back, languid, languish, languor, languorous, lassitude, lax, lay back, laze [about], lazy, leaden, lean, leisurely, lethargic, lethargy, letup, lifeless, limp, listless, loaf, loll, lounge, low-key, lull, moon[about], mope, motionless, motionlessness, nap, nod [off], out of [gas/ it], pacify, paralyzed, passive, peaceful, phlegmatic, played out, pooped, powerless, prone, prostrate, put [one's] feet up, quiescent, quiet, recess, recline, recumbent, refresh, relax, relief, relieved, repose, respite, rest, retire, run-down, rusty, sack out, sapped, sated, satiated, sawing wood, sedate, sedentary, settle, shut-eye, siesta, silent, slack, slake, sleep, sleepy, slothful, slow, sluggard, sluggish, slumber, slumped, snooze, snore, somnolent, soothe, spent, sprawl, stable, standstill, steady, still, stretch out, stupor, supine, [take a] breather, take five/ ten, tired, torpid, torpor, tranquil, tuckered [out], turn in, unhurried, unresponsive, unwind, vacant, washed out, wasted, weakened, weary, winding down, worn-out, yawning, zonked [out], zzz

See also Recline

Happily Ever After

Accept, yield

Abandon, abdicate, accede, accept, acknowledge, acquiesce, acquire, admit, admit defeat, agree, allow, assent, back down, bear, bear with, bend, bow, break, buy, capitulate, cave in, cede, collapse, come to terms, comply, concede, concur, consent, cooperate, crumbled under, crumple, defer, defer to, endure, enfold, enter into, fail, fit in, fold, fold up, gain, get, give oneself over, give the go-ahead, give the green light, give up, give way, go, go along with, grant, hand over, knuckle under, let, let go, live with, obtain, okay, permit, play the game, recognize, relax, relent, relinquish, resign, respect, sag, secure, sit still for, stand, stand for, stomach, submit, submit to, succumb, suffer, suffer defeat, surrender, swallow, take, throw in the towel, toe the line, tolerate, waive, welcome, yield, yield to

Bliss

Ardor, blessedness, bliss, buoyancy, cloud nine, contentment, delectation, delight, delirium, ebullience, ecstasy, elation, enchantment, enthusiasm, euphoria, exaltation, excitement, exhilaration, exultation, felicity, fervor, fever, frenzy, fruition, furor, fury, gladness, glee, gratification, happiness, heaven, high, high spirits, inspiration, intoxication, jollity, joy, joyousness, jubilation, kick, kicks, lunacy, mania, mirth, paradise, passion, pleasure, rapture, relish, rhapsody, satisfaction, seventh heaven, stars in one's eyes, trance, transport, triumph

Forever

Aeon, afterlife, afterward, age, ages, all one's born days, allotment, bit, blue moon, bout, by and by, chronology, clock, continuance, coon's age, date, day, destiny, dog's age, duration, endless time, endlessness, epoch, era, eternity, everlasting, expectation, extent, fate, forever, forever and a day, future, futurity, generation, go, hereafter, hour, immortality, infinite, infinitude, infinity, instance, instant, interval, juncture, kingdom come, lasting, life, life span, life to come, lifetime, long time, many a moon, millennium, moment, month, morrow, occasion, offing, other world, outlook, pace, past, perpetuity, point, posterity, present, prospect, right smart spell, season, second, shift, space, span, spell, stage, stint, stretch, subsequent time, tempo, term, tide, time immemorial, time out of mind, time without end, timelessness, to be, tomorrow, tour, turn, week, while, wild blue yonder, world to come, world without end, year, years on end

Happy

Abundance, advantage, agreeable, amiable, at ease, at home, at peace, auspicious, benevolent, blessed, blest, blissful, blithe, bright, buoyant, by good luck, by happy chance, captivated, charming, cheerful, chipper, comfortable, complacent, content, contented, contentment, conveniently, convivial, coziness, creature comforts, delighted, easygoing, ecstatic, elated, endowed, enjoyment, enthusiastic, exhilaration, exultant, favorably, favored, felicitous, flying high, fortunate, freely, gaily, glad, gleeful, golden, gracious, gratified, halcyon, happily, happiness, happy, heartily, hopeful, in good time, jolly, joyful, joyous, jubilant, laughing, lighthearted, lively, lovingly, lucky, luxury, merry, mirthful, obligingly, of good comfort, on cloud nine, optimistically, opulence, overjoyed, peaceful, perky, playful, pleasant, pleasure, plenty, politely, profitably, promising, propitious, prosperous, providence, readily, repose, rest, restfulness, rosy, satisfied, serenity, sincerely, smiling, snug, sparkling, sportive, successful, succor, sunny, swimmingly, thankful, thrilled, tickled, tickled pink, unmolested, up, upbeat, walking on air, warm, well-being, with relish, wonderfully, zestfully

Pleasure

Abundance, acceptable, action, agreeable, alleviation, alluring, amenity, amusement, appetizing, at ease, attractive, ball, beatific, beatified, bed of roses, beguilement, bewitching, blessed, blest, bliss, blissful, buzz, captivating, charming, cheer, cloudless, comfort, complacency, conciliatory, contentment, convenience, cordial, coziness, creature comforts, dainty, delectable, delectation, delicate, delicious, delight, delightful, disport, distraction, diversion, divertissement, dulcet, ease, ecstatic, Elysian, enchanting, engaging, enjoyment, enraptured, entertainment, enticing, entrancing, exhilaration, exquisite, facility, fall, fascinating, favorite, felicitous, felicity, field day, flash, frivolity, fruition, fun, fun and games, game, genial, glad, gladness, gladsome, gluttony, grateful, gratification, gusto, halcyon, happiness, happy, heartfelt, high time, hilarity, hobby, hoopla, in a blissful state, in paradise, in rapture, indulgence, inviting, joie de vivre, joyful, kicks, laughter, levity, lovely, luscious, luxury, merriment, merry go round, merry-go-round, mirth, nice, not sorry, opulence, overjoyed, palatable, pastime, peace, peace of mind, peacefulness, picnic, play, pleasant, pleased, pleasurable, plenty, poise, primrose path, quiet, recreation, relaxation, relief, relish, repose, rest, restfulness, revelry, satisfaction, seasoning, self-indulgence, snugness, solace, spice, sport, succor, sufficiency, thrill, titillation, turn-on, warmth, well-being, whoopee, zest

Promise

Affiance, affirm, affirmation, agreement, assent, assertion, assurance, attest, aver, avowal, bargain, betrothal, binding, bond, commitment, compact, confirmation, consent, contract, covenant, declaration, engagement, espousal, guarantee, insist, insure, live up to, marriage, oath, obligation, pact, pledge, plight, profess, promissory note, sacred word, say-so, secure, stipulation, string along, subscribe, swear on bible, swear up and down, take an oath, testify, token, troth, undertaking, vouch, vow, warrant, warranty, witness, word, word of honor

Sheltered

Comforting, buttoned up, cared for, cherished, complacent, contented, cozy, defended, ensconced, free from danger, guarded, harbor, home, harbored, home-free, immune, impervious, impregnable, in safety, inviolable, invulnerable, out of danger, out of harm's way, protected, reassuring, relaxed, relieved, rested, safe, safe and sound, safeguarded, secure, sheltered, shielded, sitting pretty, snug, soothed, strengthened, tended, unassailable, under lock and key, untroubled

Whole, entire

Absolute, all, bar none, complete, entire, every bit of, every single, full, greatest, intact, mass, outright, perfect, sum, thorough, total, unmitigated, unreserved, unrestricted, utmost, utter, whole

As their animosity faded, the princess and the pirate's time together on the sparkling southern ocean began to seem more serendipitous pleasure than punishment and peril. Strolling on deck one night beneath a starry cobalt sky, they were overcome by desire. Slow kisses soon melted into a passionate embrace, and they tumbled laughing onto a heap of virgin canvas.

He is...

Big

Ample, awash, beefy, big, brimming, bulky, bull, burly, capacious, chock-full, colossal, commodious, considerable, copious, crowded, cumbersome, cumbrous, enormous, extensive, fat, full, gigantic, great, heavy, heavy-duty, heavyweight, hefty, huge, hulky, hulking, humongous, husky, immense, jumbo, large, long, mammoth, massive, monster, oversize, packed, ponderous, prodigious, roomy, sizable, spacious, strapping, stout, stuffed, substantial, thick, thundering, tremendous, unwieldy, vast, voluminous, a whale of, walloping, weighty, whopper

See also Whole

Brave

Adventurous, audacious, bold, chin-up, chivalrous, confident, courageous, daring, dashing, dauntless, defiant, doughty, fearless, firm, foolhardy, forward, gallant, game, gritty, gutsy, hardy, heroic, imprudent, indomitable, intrepid, lionhearted, militant, nervy, plucky, reckless, resolute, spirited, spunky, stalwart, staunch, stouthearted, strong, unabashed, unafraid, undaunted, undismayed, valiant, valorous, venturesome

Hard

Angular, bolt upright, boner, cement-like, dense, elevated, erect, erection, firm, freestanding, granite, hard-on, hardened, heavy, immovable, impenetrable, implacable, indomitable, inexorable, inflexible, iron, marble, packed, perpendicular, plump, raised, rampant, rearing up, relentless, rigid, rising, robust, rock-like, rocky, set, solid, standing, steel, steely, stiff, stiff as a board, stiffy, stony, straight, strong, stubborn, taut, tense, thick, thickened, tight, tough, unbending, unforgiving, unyielding, upright, vertical, wooden

See also Unbending

Hero

Advocate, ally, archetype, challenger, champion, conqueror, conquistador, daredevil, darling, defeater, defender, deity, emblematic, embodiment, endorser, entrepreneur, epitome, exemplar, favorite, gauge, god, guardian, hero, iconic, ideal, image, lodestar, mold, nonpareil, number one, original, pagan symbol, paladin, paradigm, paragon, partisan, patron, pioneer, pirate, proponent, protector, prototype, quintessence, role model, romantic, saint, stunt person, superstar hero, supporter, swashbuckler, symbol, sympathizer, the greatest, titleholder, top dog, touchstone, upholder, vanquisher, victor, vindicator, warrior, winner

Handsome, masculine

Admirable, alluring, angelic, ape, appealing, aristocratic, athletic, attractive, audacious, august, beauteous, beautiful, becoming, beefcake, bold, brave, caveman, charming, classy, clean-cut, comely, confident, courageous, cute, dapper, daring, dazzling, delightful, dignified, divine, elegant, enticing, excellent, exquisite, fair, fearless, fine, firm, foxy, gallant, generative, good-looking, gorgeous, graceful, grand, hairy, handsome, hardy, he-man, heroic, honorable, hot, hunk, ideal, impressive, intrepid, jock, macho, magnificent, majestic, male, manlike, manliness, manly, marvelous, masculine, muscular, noble, potent, powerful, pretty, radiant, ravishing, red-blooded, resolute, resplendent, robust, self-reliant, shapely, sightly, splendid, stallion, stately, strapping, strong , studly, stunning, stylish, suave, sublime, superb, symmetrical, taking, tiger, two-fisted, vigorous, virile, well-built, well-dressed, well-formed, well-proportioned, wonderful

Skillful, experienced

Able, accomplished, accustomed, adapted, adept, adroit, apt, artistic, been around, been there, brainy, brilliant, broken in, capable, clever, competent, consummate, cultivated, cut out for, dynamite, efficient, endowed, experienced, expert, familiar, fireball, fitted, gifted, good, has what it takes, having a knack, know-how , in the know, ingenious, instructed, intelligent, know the ropes/ score, a pistol, masterly, mature, old hand, old-timer, on the ball, polished, practiced, pro, professional, proficient, proper, qualified, rounded, savvy, seasoned, sharp, skilled, skillful, smart, sophisticated, sport, talented, tested, the right stuff, there, trained, tried, up to it, up to snuff, up to speed, versed, vet, veteran, well-suited, well-versed, wise, with it, worldly, worldly-wise

Strong

Able-bodied, active, adept, adequate, adroit, agile, athletic, beefcake, beefy, big, brawny, bruising, bulky, capable, compelling, competent, convincing, cunning, definition, deft, dexterous, distinct, durable, easy, effortless, endowed, enduring, energetic, equipped, eye-catching, fast, firm, fit, forceful, formidable, gorilla-like, hale, hard as nails, hardy, healthy, hearty, heavy, heavy-duty, hefty, hulking, hunk, husky, in fine feather, influential, lusty, mighty, muscular, overpowering, persuasive, portly, potent, powerful, prominent/pronounced muscles, ready, redoubtable, robust, rugged, sharp, sinewy, solid, sound, stable, stalwart, staunch, steady, stiff, stimulating, stocky, stout, strapping, strong, sturdy, substantial, tenacious, thickset, tough, unyielding, vigorous, well-built

Aware of the terrible fate she'd face should her villanous stepfather or afianced groom discover her disgrace, the princess nonetheless could not resist the handsome pirate. His leisurely kisses and gentle strokes along her spine seduced her, despite the tingle of apprehension she felt when he disrobed.

She is...

Active, blunt, delicate, divine, emerging, enticing, exaggerated, extended, firm, handing, hanging, hard as a pebble, heavy-lidded, hot flesh, hung down, inflamed, jutting, out-thrust, pendulous, pert, pointed, provocative, puffy, raw, resilient, rigid, ripe, silky smooth, stiffened, succulent, swell, swelling, swollen, tapering, taut, tender, thick, undersides, upper, vulnerable, waiting, warm

Beautiful, feminine

Admirable, adorable, agreeable, airy, alluring, amiable, amusing, attractive, beauteous, beautiful, beckoning, bewitching, bonny, captivating, charming, cheery, choice, clever, comely, congenial, consummate, cultivated, cute, dainty, darling, delectable, delicate, delicious, delightful, diaphanous, effeminate, elegant, enchanting, engaging, enjoyable, entertaining, enthralling, enticing, ethereal, exquisite, fair, fascinating, fastidious, fecund, female, feminine, fertile, fetching, fine, flawless, frail, glamorous, good-looking, gorgeous, graceful, handsome, heavenly, impeccable, incomparable, ineffable, interesting, inviting, knockout, lacy, ladylike, light, looker, lovely, luscious, lush, magnetic, matchless, maternal, mesmeric, meticulous, neat, nice, outstanding, palatable, peerless, perfect, picture of, pleasant, pleasing, polished, precious, precise, prepossessing, pretty, provocative, rapturous, rare, ravishing, refined, refreshing, satisfying, savory, scrumptious, seductive, selective, soft, splendid, striking, stunning, subtle, superb, superior, superlative, sweet, tantalizing, tasteful, tasty, tempting, thrilling, toothsome, trim, well-made, winning, winsome, womanly, yummy

Delicate

Aerial, balmy, breakable, choice, dainty, delectable, delicious, delightful, elegant, ethereal, exquisite, faint, filmy, fine, fine-grained, finespun, flimsy, fragile, frail, frangible, gauzy, gossamery, graceful, mild, muted, nice, pale, pastel, rare, select, slight, subdued, subtle, tender, weak

See also Sexy Clothing Words

Gentle

Affable, affectionate, agreeable, amiable, benign, biddable, bland, compassionate, considerate, cool, courteous, cultivated, docile, dove-like, easy, easy-going, effortless, genial, gentle, gracious, humane, indulgent, kind, kindly, laid back, lax, lenient, liberal, manageable, meek, mellow, merciful, mild-natured, overindulgent, pacific, pacifistic, peaceful, permissive, pitying, placid, pleasant, pleasing, pliable, quiet, sensitive, sentimental, simple, soft, softhearted, spineless, sweet-tempered, sympathetic, tame, taught, temperate, tender, tender-hearted, tractable, undemanding, warmhearted, weak

Smooth, soft

Bendable, bland, comfortable, comfy, compliant, continuous, cottony, cozy, creamy, cushiony, cushy, delicate, doughy, downy, ductile, easy, effortless, elastic, even, feathery, fine, flabby, flat, fleecy, fleshy, flexible, flimsy, flowing, fluent, fluffy, fluid, flush, forgiving, formless, frictionless, furry, gelatinous, gentle, glassy, glossy, hairless, horizontal, impressible, invariable, limp, lustrous, malleable, mild, moldable, monotonous, mushy, pappy, peaceful, pithy, plain, plane, plastic, pliable, polished, pulpy, quiet, receptive, regular, rounded, satiny, serene, shiny, silken, silky, sleek, smooth, soft, spongy, squishy, supple, tractable, tranquil, unbroken, undisturbed, uniform, uninterrupted, unresisting, unruffled, unvarying, velvety, yielding

Tight

Adhere, binding, boxed in, casing, chamber, cherish, clamp, clasp, clasped, cleave to, clinch, close, close-fitting, closed in, clutching, compact, confined, constricted, contracted, crabbed, cramped, crowded, diminutive, drawn, embrace, endure, enfold, enveloping, fasten, firm, fixed, fold into, grapple, grasp, grip, hemmed in, hold, hold fast, hug, inadequate, inflexible, jammed in, limited, linger, little, meager, minute, narrow, negligible, packed, paltry, pent-up, pinching, press, pressure, restricted, rigid, scabbard, secure, seize, set, sheath, skimpy, skintight, slender, slight, small, snug, spare, sparse, squeezing, stiff, strained, stretched, strong, taut, tenacious, tense, thick, thin, tight, tightened, tiny, tucked in, unbending, uncomfortable, unyielding, wrapper, wrapping

See also Yield

Virginal

Above suspicion, adorable, amateur, angelic, artless, beatific, beneficent, celestial, chaste, cherubic, clean, clear, crimeless, devout, direct, divine, entrancing, ethereal, exemplary, faultless, free of, fresh, genuine, godly, good, green, guileless, guilt-free, guiltless, heavenly, honest, immaculate, impeccable, in the clear, inculpable, inept, inexperienced, inexpert, ingenuous, innocent, irreproachable, naive, natural, new, not versed in, otherworldly, pristine, pure, radiant, rapturous, raw, righteous, rookie, saintly, self-sacrificing, seraphic, simple, sincere, sinless, spotless, stainless, straight, straightforward, tenderfoot, unaccustomed, unacquainted, unadorned, unaffected, unblemished, unconversant, uncorrupted, undisciplined, uneducated, unfamiliar with, unimpeachable, uninformed, unlearned, unlettered, unmarked, unpracticed, unpretentious, unschooled, unseasoned, unsophisticated, unsullied, untainted, untaught, untouched, untrained, untried, untutored, unwitting, unworldly, up front, upright, virgin, virginal, virtuous, void, wet behind ears

See also Puritanical

Surprised by her innocent ardor, the
pirate was nearly unable to restrain himself,
but his patient and skillful caresses opened her eyes
to the world of exquisite sensations awaiting her. The princess'
unschooled undulations were more arousing to him than the most
experienced courtesan and when at last he abandoned himself,
they were swept helplessly into a binding whirlpool of delight.

Body Parts & Descriptions

See also Hair & Skin, Non-specific descriptors

Area

Area, branch, breadth, bridge, dimension, distance, expansion, extension, extent, gamut, junction, length, orbit, proliferation, purview, radius, range, reach, region, scope, space, span, spread, sweep, tract, wing

Bits & Pieces

Mouth, lips, tongue, throat, oral

See also Taste

Waist, abdomen, abs, belly, belt, girth, gut, middle, midriff, midsection, paunch, potbelly, ribcage, spare tire, stomach, torso, tummy

Pelvis, crotch, flanks, groin, haunch, hips, junction, juncture, lap, loins, lower body, saddle, thighs

See also Between

Flesh, assets, cheek, core, goosebumps, membrane, muscles, privates, skin, tentacle, toes curled, zone

Blunt, delicate, divine, emerging, enticing, exaggerated, extended, firm, handing, hanging, hard as a pebble, heavy-lidded, hot, hung down, inflamed, jutting, out-thrust, pendulous, pert, pointed, provocative, puffy, raw, resilient, rigid, ripe, rounded, silky smooth, stiffened, succulent, swelling, swollen, tapering, taut, tender, thick, undersides, upper, vulnerable, waiting, warm

Breasts

Areolas, boobs, bosom, buds, chest, cleavage, crest, globes, heaving, hill, hooters, jugs, mams, mounds, nubs, slope, summits, teats, tips, tit-flesh, tits

Bottom

Anal, anus, ass, backside, behind, bottom, bowels, buns, butt, buttocks, can, cheeks, crease, derriere, dimpled hole, fanny, glutes, gluteus maximus, heinie, hole, keister, moon, posterior, pucker, rear, rear end, rear passage, rectum, ring of muscle, rump, seat, sphincter, tail, tuchis, tush/ y, wrinkled opening

Cleft or opening

Aperture, arroyo, basin, bayou, box, breach, break, brim, burrow, canyon, carving, cave, cavern, cavity, chamber, chasm, chink, chip, chop, cleavage, cleft, clove, concave, cove, covert, crack, cranny, crater, crevasse, crevice, cut, defile, delta, dent, dimple, dip, divide, division, door, entrance, entry, estuary, excavation, faction, fault, fiord, firth, fissure, flaw, fracture, funnel, furrow, gap, gash, gate, gorge, groove, gulch, gulf, gully, harbor, hole, hollow, incision, inlet, inner curve, lagoon, lair, mouth, narrows, nest, niche, nick, nip, notch, opening, orifice, outlet, passage, perforation, pit, portal, ravine, recess, rent, rift, rim, rip, rupture, schism, scoop, section, separation, severance, shaft, shelter, slash, slit, slot, sound, space, split, spout, strait, stroke, trench, tunnel, valley, void, window, wound

Fingers, hands

Callused, digits, fingernails, fingertips, fist, heel of hand, knuckles, nails, palm, pad at base of fingers

See also Touch. Skillful, Soft, Easily

Penis

Arrow, balls, bar, bat, bulge, chimney, club, cock, column, crown, cylinder, dick, erection, handle, hard-on, head, helmet, hilt, lance, log, meat, missile, obelisk, penis, phallus, pillar, pipe, piston, plank, pole, prick, prong, ramrod, rod, root, shaft, spear, staff, stalk, stem, stiletto, sword, tip, tool, woody, scrotum

See also He is…, Hard, Big, Swollen

Vagina

Bush, canal, cervix, channel, clitoral hood, pussy, clit, labia core, cunny, cunt, depths, flower, folds, g-spot, gash, her sex, hymen, inner lips, labia, lips, love button, bud, maidenhead, melons, mound, mouth of, nodule, nub, nubbin of flesh, opening, passage, petals, puss, quim, ridge, sheath, slash, slit, snatch, tunnel, twat, vagina, vulva, womb

See also Wet, Tight, Color

Non-specific descriptors

Abundant, affluent, ambrosial, ample, bantam, barren, beanpole, beefy, big, bird-like, blimp, blowsy, blubber, bony, bouncy, bounteous, bountiful, bovine, bowed, brawny, broad, bulbous, bulging, bulky, bull, burgeoning, burly, butterball, cadaverous, cellulite, chubby, chunky, clean, compact, copious, corpulent, curled, curves, deflated, delectable, delicate, delicious, deluxe, dense, depleted, destitute, developing, dilating, diminutive, distended, dome, drained, dumpy, effete, egg-shaped, elephantine, emaciated, ethereal, excess, exhausted, expanding, expansive, extending, extravagant, fading, failing, fat, fecund, fertile, filling out, flab, flesh, fleshy, flourishing, fragile, fresh, frumpy, full, gangly, gargantuan, gaunt, generous, giant, globe, globular, grand, growing, haggard, heavy, heavyset, hefty, hollow, hulking, husky, immense, impoverished, inadequate, inflated, insubstantial, itty-bitty, juicy, lacking, laden, lank, lanky, large, lavish, lean, liberal, lightweight, Lilliputian, little, luscious, lush, luxuriant, malnourished, massive, mature, meager, meaty, microscopic, mini, miniature, miniscule, minute, modest, narrow frame, needy, negligible, obese, orb, orbicular, oval, overabundant, overgrown, overweight, paunchy, peaked, peewee, perky, pert, petite, pint-sized, plenty, plump, plumpish, plush, pole, ponderous, portly, pot-bellied, prolific, prosperous, pudgy, puny, rangy, rarefied, rawboned, reedy, rich, riotous, ripe, roly-poly, rotund, rounded, runt, sag, scanty, scarce, scrawny, scrumptious, shadow of, short, shrimp, shrinking, shriveled, shrunken, skeletal, skimpy, skinny, slender, slight, slim, small, soaring, solid, spare, spent, spherical, spindly, spreading, squat, stable, stalk, starved, statuesque, stick, stout, strapping, stretching, stubby, stunted tiny, sturdy, substantial, succulent, sumptuous, surplus, swelling, teeming, teeny, tender, thick, thickset, thin, thriving, tired, towering, tubby, twig-like, undernourished, undersized, underweight, verdant, voluptuous, wan, wanting, wasted, wasting away, weighty, whale, withered, wrinkled

See also Bits & Pieces

Hair & Skin

Airy, bald, beard/ed, blanket, bright, brilliant, bristle, bristling, bristly, brush/ y, burnished, bushy, cape, cilium, cloak, coat, cobweb, cascaded, clumps, coiffure, cottony, cover, cowlick, delicate, diaphanous, dome, down/y, drab, dull, eyebrow, eyelash, feather-like, feathery, fiber, fibrous, filament, fine, fleecy, flimsy, fluff/y, fringe, fringed, frizzies, full, fur/ry, fuzz/y, glassy, glazed, gleaming, glistening, glossy, gossamer, grass, greasy, hair, haircut, hairstyle, hairy, heavy, hirsute, kinky, lanugo, light, limp, lifeless, lustrous, luxuriant, luxurious, mane, mop, moustache/d, nap/py, parka, pelt/ed, plush, polished, prickly, pubescent, quill, reflecting, rough, ruff, rumpled, satin/y, satiny, shaggy, shawl, sheer, shiny, shock of hair, sideburns, silk/y, silken, sleek, slick, smooth, soft, split ends, spreading, stiff, strands, thatch, thick, threads, thicket, tresses, tuft/ed, unkempt, unruly, velvety, vibrant, waxy, whiskers, wig, wiry, wool/ly, tufted

See also Smooth

Hair Styles

Afro, bangs, beehive, blow dry, bob, bouffant, braid, braided, brush-cut, bun, chignon, buzz-cut, carpet, chignon, coiffure, comb-over, corn-rows, crew-cut, cropped, curly, cut, 'do, Dorothy Hamill, dreadlocks, dreads, duck-tail, Dutch braid, fade, feather cut, flat-top, flattop, flip, French braid, fuzz cut, haircut, hairdo, horse tail, long, mohawk, natural, pageboy, patch, rug, permanent, pigtails, pixie, plait, pompadour, D.A., ponytail, Rachel, razor cut, sealskin, shag, short, slicked back, gelled, springy, straight, tail, tease, tendrils, trim, upswept, wavy, weave, widow's peak

Facial Hair

Anchor, brushy, chinstrap, circle beard, clean-shaven, five o'clock shadow, Franz Josef, French fork, Fu Manchu, goatee, handlebar, horseshoe mustache, Magnum PI, monkey tail, mutton chops, peach fuzz, pencil mustache, soul patch, 'stash, stubble, Van Dyke, Zappa, 70s porn

Pubic hair

Peach fuzz, landing strip, trim, bush, natural, Brazilian, waxed, French wax, Hollywood wax, clean-shaven, landing strip, triangle, merkin

Color- Skin or Hair

Alabaster, amber, anemic, ash, auburn, balayage, bay, beige, berry-brown, biscuit, black, blanched, bleached, blonde, bloodless, blotchy, brassy, brick, bronze, brown, brunette, brunette, butterscotch, buff, burnt sienna, café au lait, camel, caramel, chalky, champagne, charcoal, chestnut, chocolate, cinnamon, clear, coal, cocoa, coffee, colorless, complexion, copper, cream, dapple, dirty blonde, dishwater, drab, dusky, dust, dusty, ebony, ecru, faded, fair, fawn, fiery, flaxen, foxy, frosted, ghastly, ginger, glow, golden, gray, hazel, henna, highlights, honey, honeyed, ink, ivory, jet, khaki, leaden, light, mahogany, marbled, maroon, milky, mousy, murky, mushroom, neutral, nut, oak leaf, oatmeal, obsidian, ashen, ochre, off-white, olive, ombre, straw, pale, pallid, pasty, pearly, pigmentation, platinum, raven, red, russet, rust, sable, sallow, salt-and-pepper, sand, sandy, seal, sepia, silver, slate, snowy, sooty, sorrel, strawberry blonde, sunburned, swarthy, tan, tanned, taupe, tawny, terra-cotta, titian, toast, tortoiseshell, towheaded, umber, wan, waxen, blanched, wheat, white, variegated

Skin (blushing, illness, other)

Afterglow, apple, ashen, awash, aglow, be suffused, black-and-blue, blare, blazing, bloom, blossom, bluish, blush, brighten, brilliance, bruised, burn, cadaverous, chartreuse, color, color up, coral, crimson, darken, deathly, fill, flaming, flare, flecked, florid, flushed, freckled, fuchsia, gleam, glimmer, glisten, glitter, glow, go red, greenish, ignite, jade, jaundiced, kindle, lavender, light, lime, livid, luminous, mantle, maroon, mauve, mottled, mulberry, olive, passion, pea, pink, pinken, plum, purple, radiant, red, redden, rose, rosy, rouge, salmon, shine, smolder, suffuse, thrill, tingle, tint, twinkle, undertone, violet, warmth, wash, wine, yellow

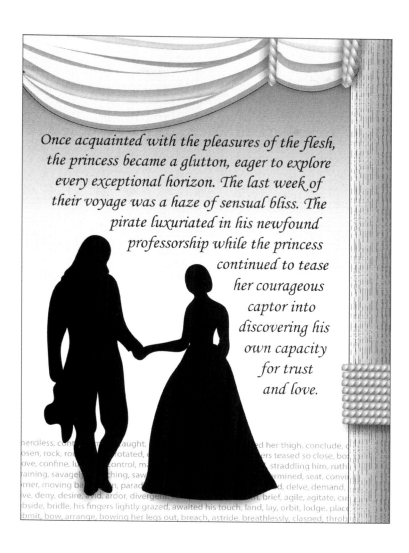

Once acquainted with the pleasures of the flesh,
the princess became a glutton, eager to explore
every exceptional horizon. The last week of
their voyage was a haze of sensual bliss. The
pirate luxuriated in his newfound
professorship while the princess
continued to tease
her courageous
captor into
discovering his
own capacity
for trust
and love.

merciless, con... ...aught, ...d her thigh, conclude, ...
...osen, rock, ro... ...otated, ...ers teased so close, bo...
...ove, confine, l... ...ontrol, m... ...straddling him, ruth...
...aining, savage... ...hing, saw... ...rmined, seat, convi...
...ner, moving ba... ...n, parad... ...d, delve, demand, ...
...ve, deny, desire, avid, ardor, diverge... ...t, brief, agile, agitate, cu...
...bside, bridle, his fingers lightly grazed, awaited his touch, land, lay, orbit, lodge, plac...
...bmit, bow, arrange, bowing her legs out, breach, astride, breathlessly, clasped, throb...

Logistics, physical position

Adapt, change

Alter, become, change, change into, come, convert, divert, fashion, fit, form, get, go, grow into, metamorphose, modify, mold, mutate, pass into, put, refashion, remake, remodel, render, run, re/shape, transfigure, transform, translate, transmute, transpose, vary, wax

See also New, different, Yield

Between

Amid, amidst, among, at intervals, average, between, betwixt, bounded by, center, centermost, centrally located, enclosed by, equidistant, halfway, in the middle, in the midst of, in the seam, inner, inserted, inside, intermediate, interpolated, intervening, mainstream, mean, medial, median, medium, middle of the road, middlemost, midmost, midway, separating, smack in the middle, straddling the fence, surrounded by, 'tween, within

See also Body Parts (Pelvis)

Bordering, edge

Abut, adjoin, be adjacent to, bend, berm, bind, bound, boundary, brim, brink, butt, circumference, circumscribe, communicate, contour, corner, crook, crust, curb, decorate, define, delineate, edge, encircle, enclose, end, extremity, flank, frame, fringe, frontier, hem, hook, join, ledge, limb, limit, line, lip, march, margin, mark off, molding, mouth, neighbor, outline, outskirt, peak, perimeter, periphery, point, portal, rim, ring, set off, shore, side, skirt, split, strand, surround, term, threshold, tip, touch, trim, trimming, turn, verge

In relation to

About, above, abut, adjoin, all over, any which way, approach, around, at the end, band, be adjacent to, be on the edge, behind, bending, beneath, beset, beside, between, blanketed, block, bordered, bound, bound to, brace, butt on, buttress, cage, circle, circumference, circumscribed, closed in, coiled around, concealed, confined, contain, contiguous, contour, cooped, corkscrew, corral, covered, curled around, decorate, defined, delimited, delineate, draped, edged, embrace, encase, encircled, enclosed, encompassed by, encompassing, enfold, engulf, enmesh, enshrouded, entangle, entrenched, entwine, enveloped, everywhere, fasten, fenced, finite, flanked, fortify, frame, fringed, girdled, guard, halo, hedged in, hem in, hide, hinder, immure, in back of, in front of, in the area/ vicinity, in the environ, interlace, intertwine, interwoven, joined, knit, lace, lining, looped, margin, neighboring, obscure, obstruct, on the edge, outlining, over, penned, protected, restricted, rimmed, ringed, roll, round, secure, set off, sheathed, shield, shroud, shut in, side, siege, situated on sides, skirting, spiraling, superimposed, support, surrounded, swaddle, swathe, tangle, throughout, touching, twine, twisted around, under, underneath, undulate, verging on, walled, weave, wind, wrapped up, wreathed in

Lift, move up

Arise, bear, bear aloft, boost, bring, build up, buoy up, burden, carry, cart, climb, come up, conduct, convey, displace, draw up, elevate, erect, ferry, fetch, freight, give, haul, heft, hike, hoist, jack up, jump up, lift, lug, mount, move, pack, pick up, portage, prop, put up, raise, rising up, rear, relay, relocate, remove, rise, schlepp, shift, shoulder, soar, sustain, take up, tote, transmit, transport, truck, uphold, uplift, upraise

Support (weight)

Balance on, bear, bolster, brace, cantilever, carry, cushion, foothold, footing, fulcrum, hold, hold up, kneel, lug, perch, pillow, prop, purchase, recline, rely, rest on, ride, settle, sit, stance, stand, straddle, support, toehold

Recline, relax, lean

Arced, arched up, bent, bow, breathe easy, bum, calm down, cant, careen, [catch one's] breath, chill out, cock, collected, composed, cool off, curve, dangle, dawdle, decline, deflect, dip, divert, double up, drift, droop, drop, fasten on, feel at home, flap, flop, go to bed, goof off, hang, hang loose, idle, incline, lay down, laze, lean, lie, list, loaf, loiter, loll, loosen up, lounge, make oneself at home, mellow out, nap, nod, off duty, pitch, place, plop down, prone, prop, put one's feet up, recline, recumbent, relax, repose, rest, rest on, retire, roll, sag, settle back, sheer, siesta, sink, sit around, sit back, slant, slanted, sleep, slope, slouch, slump, sprawl, stretch/ out, supine, take a break/ breather, take a load off, take it easy, take ten, tilt, tip, turn in, unwind, veg, wind down

See also Relaxed

Turn, reverse

About-face, aim, alter, alternate, angle, arc, backslide, bend, bias, bow, branch off, call off, capsize, change, change course, circle, circuit, circulate, circumduct, come around, convert, corner, curve, cut away/ toward, cycle, depart, departure, detour, deviate, digress, direction, diverge, double back, drift, eddy, flexure, fork, go around, go back, gyrate, hang a left/ right, heading, hook, incline, invert, loop, make a left/ right, move, move in a circle, negotiate, orbit, oscillate, pass, pirouette, pivot, quirk, recoil, redirect, regress, relapse, retrace, return, reverse, revert, revolve, right-about, roll, rotate, rotation, round, sheer, shift, shunt, shy away, sidetrack, spin, spiral, subvert, sway, swerve, swing, swing around/ about, swirl, switch tack, swivel, tack, tendency, transform, trend, turnabout, turning, twirl, twist, upset routine, vary, veer, wheel, whip, whirl, wind, winding, yaw, zigzag

See also Repeat

Dreading their arrival and the horror sure to follow, the princess was instead astonished to find that her handsome pirate is a wealthy duke in his spare time. He sent the evil fiance packing, vanquished the princess' wicked stepfather and freed her grateful sisters from their interminable imprisonment.

Roughing it

Authority, compel

Ascendancy, assert, authorization, bear down, browbeat, bulldoze, charge ahead, clout, coerce, command, constrain, control, domination, dominion, dragoon, egg on, encourage, enslave, exert influence, expedite, fire up, force, go to town on, goad, goose, guts, hurry, impel, influence, inspire, intimidate, jolly, jurisdiction, key up, kid, lean on, leg up, mastery, might, motivate, oblige, overpower, permission, permit, persuade, pour it on, powerhouse, prerogative, press, pressure, prod, punch, push around, put the screws to, put up to, railroad, rule, say-so, sell on, speed up, spur, squeeze, steam ahead, steamroll, strength, strong arm, strong-arm, subjugate, supremacy, sway, take over, throw weight around, turn on, upper hand, urge, warrant

Courtesan

Admirer, bawd, call girl, camp follower, concubine, courtesan, doxy, escort, fallen woman, floozy, girlfriend, harlot, hooker, hussy, hustler, kept woman, lady of the evening, lady of the night, light skirt, loose woman, mistress, moll, painted woman, pro, prostitute, scarlet woman, slut, streetwalker, strumpet, tart, tramp, trollop, whore, woman of the streets, working girl

Despoiled, ruined

Abase, abuse, abused, adulterated, assaulted, bastardize, blemish, contaminate, damage, debase, debauchery, decay, deface, defiled, deflowered, degrade, demeaning, demoralize, deprave, depreciate, depredation, deprive, desecrate, despoil, despoiled, destroy, devastate, devour, disfigure, disgrace, dishonored, dispossess, forced, harm, hurt, ill-treatment, infect, injure, looted, lower, maltreated, marred, maraud, mistreat, misused, pillage, plunder, raid, raped, ravage, ravished, reduce, rifle, ruined, sack, spoiled, stain, subversion, taint, undermine, vandalize, violated, waste, wreak havoc, wreck

Evil

Angry, atrocious, awry, bad, baneful, base, beastly, calamitous, corrupt, criminal, damnable, deadly, delinquent, depraved, deprecatory, destructive, devilish, diabolic, dire, disastrous, evil, execrable, foreboding, foul, harmful, hateful, heinous, hell, hideous, hurtful, immoral, iniquitous, injurious, loathsome, low, maleficent, malevolent, malicious, malignant, mean, nefarious, no good, noxious, obscene, offensive, ominous, pernicious, poison, rancorous, reprobate, repugnant, repulsive, revolting, ruinous, satanic, sinful, sinister, spiteful, stinking, threatening, ugly, unpleasant venal, venomous, vicious, vile, villainous, vindictive, wicked, wrathful, wrong

Grab, get

Abduct, access, achieve, acquirement, acquisition, amass, annex, apprehend, appropriate, appropriation, arrest, attain, bag, bring in, capture, catch, catch hold of, clap, clinch, clutch, collar, collect, commandeer, confiscate, cop, corral, ensnaring, gain, gather, get, grab, grapple, grasp, grip, hijack, hold, hook, land, latch onto, lay one's hands on, lock up, nab, nail, obtain, pick up, pinch, pluck, procure, reign in, seize, snag,'s snatch, sweep, take, take hold of, take over, take possession of, trap, usurp, win

Hold, control

Adhere, anchor, be true to, brace, catch, cherish, cinch, clamp, clamp down, clasp, cleave to, clench, clinch, clutch, command, constrain, control, crushing, domineer, dominion, embrace, enclose, enclosure, fasten, fastening, fixing, get one's hands on, grapple with, grasp, grip, handhold, hang onto, hold fast, hook, hug, keep, latch on to, lay hands on, mastery, nab, occupy, own, possess, pull, purchase, restrain, retention, seize, snag, snatch, squeeze, stay put, stick, take, take hold of, tenacity, vise, wrench, secure, talons, rule, sway, reign, wield, suppress

Puritanical

Abstemious, abstinent, ascetic, austere, bourgeois, chaste, cleanly, conservative, conventional, correct, decorous, demure, doctrinal, dogmatic, fastidious, formal, genteel, goody-goody, goody-two-shoes, hidebound, illiberal, inflexible, moral, narrow-minded, nit-picking, overmodest,, persnickety, picky, precious, priggish, prim, prim and proper, prissy, proper, prosaic, prudish, puritanical, refraining, rigid, self-denying, self-disciplined, sissy, sober, solemn, square, squeamish, stern, stickler, stiff, straight-laced, strict, stuffy, subdued, tight-laced, upright, uptight, Victorian, wooden

See also Virginal

Ravage

Annihilate, appropriate, burglarize, capture, consume, cream, crush, demolish, desolate, despoil, destroy, devastate, dismantle, explore, extinguish, forage, foray, go through, grab, hunt, lay waste, leave in ruins, lift, loot, make off with, maraud, overrun, overthrow, overwhelm, pilfer, pillage, pinch, pirate, plunder, poach, prey, probe, pull down, purloin, raid, rake, ransack, rape, ravish, raze, rifle, rip, rob, ruin, rummage, rustle, sack, scan, scour, scrutinize, search, seek, seize, shatter, sink, smash, spoil, steal, strip, sweep away, take, tear, thieve, trample, waste, wreak havoc, wreck, wrest

Rough (manners, sound, & sensation)

Abrading, abrasive, acerbic, annoying, astringent, austere, barbaric, biting, bitter, bleak, boorish, brutish, cacophonous, calculous, caterwauling, caustic, clashing, coarse, corroding, cracked, craggy, crass, creaking, croaking, croaky, crude, crumbly, cursory, cutting, disagreeing, discordant, dissonant, disturbing, dry, dusty, earsplitting, earthy, erosive, flat, formless, friable, galling, glaring, grainy, grating, gravelly, grim, grinding, gruff, guttural, hard, harsh, hoarse, husky, imperfect, in particles, incompatible, inelegant, jagged, jangling, jarring, lumpy, mordant, nasty, noisy, off-key, out-of-key, out-of-tune, porous, powdery, primitive, ransack, rasping, raspy, raucous, raw, rigid, rough, rough-and-ready, rough-hewn, rude, rudimentary, rugged, rusty, sandy, scratching, scratchy, screech, scuff, severe, shapeless, sharp, sharpening, sketchy, smoothing, sour, spartan, spiky, squawk, strident, thick, throaty, tuneless, uncivilized, uncompleted, uncouth, uncultivated, uncultured, uncut, undressed, uneven, unfeeling, unfinished, unformed, ungracious, unmannerly, unpleasant, unpolished, unprocessed, unrefined, unsophisticated, untutored, vulgar

Sassy, rude

Aggressive, annoying, antagonizing, arrant, assuming, audacious, bad-mannered, barefaced, bold, boorish, brash, brassy, brazen, brusque, cavalier, challenging, cheeky, churlish, coming on strong, confident, crude, crusty, curt, daring, defiant, discourteous, disobedient, disrespectful, flip, flippant, forward, fresh, gritty, gutsy, ill-bred, ill-mannered, immodest, impertinent, impudent, indelicate, insolent, insubordinate, mouthy, mutinous, nervy, oafish, obstinate, offhand, overbold, pert, presumptuous, provocative, rebellious, recalcitrant, reckless, refractory, resistant, rude, rustic, sassy, saucy, shameless, smart, smart-alecky, smart-mouthed, spunky, teasing, truculent, uncivil, uncouth, ungracious, unmannerly, unrefined, wise

Ruffian, villain

Adversary, animal, antagonist, antihero, arch enemy, assailant, assassin, attacker, backbiter, bad person, bandit, beast, betrayer, black sheep, blackguard, brigand, bruiser, brute, bulldozer, bully, bum, cad, cannibal, cheat, competitor, contender, convict, coward, creature, creep, criminal, critter, crook, cutthroat, dealer, defamer, defiler, degenerate, delinquent, desperado, detractor, devil, dog, evil, evildoer, falsifier, felon, fiend, foe, gangster, good-for-nothing, goon, guerrilla, gunman, harrier, hector, heel, hellion, highwayman, hijacker, hit person, holdup person, hood, hoodlum, hooligan, hound, imp, incubus, informer, inquisitor, insolent, invader, knave, lawbreaker, libertine, little devil, lout, lowlife, mafioso, malefactor, malignant spirit, marauder, mercenary, member of the family, mischief-maker, miscreant, mobster, monster, mugger, murderer, ne'er-do-well, offender, ogre, opponent, opportunist, opposition, oppressor, other side, outlaw, persecutor, pest, pilferer, pillager, pirate, plunderer, profligate, psychopath, punk, pusher, racketeer, raider, rapscallion, rascal, rat, ravager, rebel, reprobate, revolutionary, riffraff, rioter, rival, robber, rogue, rowdy, ruffian, saboteur, sadist, Satan, savage, scoundrel, scum, shark, shyster, sinner, skunk, slanderer, snake, sociopath, spy, stinker, succubus, swindler, swine, tease, terrorist, thug, toad, tormenter, tough, tough guy, traducer, traitor, troublemaker, vampire, villain, worm, wretch, yellow dog

Shocking

Abominable, alarming, appalling, astonishing, astounding, atrocious, awesome, awful, bad, breathtaking, confounding, daunting, desperate, detestable, dire, disgraceful, disgusting, disheartening, dismaying, disquieting, distressing, dreadful, eye-popping, fascinating, fearful, formidable, foul, frightening, frightful, ghastly, glaring, grim, gross, harrowing, hateful, heavy , heinous, hideous, horrible, horrid, horrific, horrifying, incredible, intimidating, loathsome, mean, mind-blowing, mind-boggling, monstrous, nauseating, odious, offensive, overwhelming, petrifying, prodigious, repulsive, revolting, scandalous, scaring, shameful, shocking, sickening, startling, stunning, stupefying, surprising, terrible, terrifying, unbelievable, unnerving, unspeakable, wondrous

See also Naughty

Unbending (personality)

Adamant, anchored, attached, bolted, braced, cemented, constant, cruel, dead set/ on, determined, dogged, dug in, embedded, established, fast, firm, fixed, hard, hard-nosed, harsh, hell bent/ on, immobile, immovable, immutable, implacable, inescapable, inexorable, inflexible, intransigent, ironclad, locked, locked into, merciless, motionless, obdurate, obstinate, permanent, pitiless, quiescent, relentless, resolute, rigid, riveted, rooted, secure, set, set in stone, settled, single-minded, situated, solid, sound, spiked, stable, staunch, steadfast, steady, still, strong, stubborn, stuck, sturdy, substantial, tenacious, tough nut, unalterable, unbending, unchangeable, uncompromising, unmovable, unmoving, unrelenting, unshakable, unwavering, unyielding

See also Hard

The Dark Side

Abuse, accentuate, advantage, afraid, against her will, animal, anticipation, assault, bindings, bolder, bondage, bound, brace [oneself], brazenly, bruising, brunt, brutal, brutally, buried, burned, capacity, chains, chastise, coax, collar, command, compliant, complied, compressing, concealed, concentrated on, confronted, connected, continued, continuously, control, cornered, crude, cuff, dawning, deep, deeper, defenseless, delay, demanding, destination, devastating, dirty, dodging, domineering, dragging, draped it, edges, elastic, electrifying, encounter, endure, escaping, evade, expand, experience, explode, exposed, extreme, eyeing, farther, faster, fear, fiercely, filthy, forbidden, force, fought, friction, fruitless, fury, gaping, glistening, grossly exposed, harass, harder, heaved, higher, hold back, horny, humiliated, humiliation, incredulous, inevitable, intrusion, invading, kneeling, lascivious, leer, lewd, mammoth, merciless, mercy, metal, ministrations, nakedness, naughty, obey, obeying, obscene, onslaught, oppose, ordered, overstimulated, overwhelmed, packed, pain, panting, passivity, penetrated, penned up, pent up, perform, perverse, pinch, pinned down, pinned tightly together, pistoning, plunge, pointed, pound, powerful, pre-cum, prevent, prolong, protest, punishment, raining down, rapidly, rapture, reaching out, react, recently violated, reciprocate, reconciled, redoubled, resistance, resisting, response, riding, ripped, risk, rock hard, rope, savage, scandalous, scared, seedy, seething, sensation, session, shame, shamelessly, sharp, shot his load, shoved in, shriveled, slammed, slap, smutty, sodomize, spanked, spanking, spectacle, spunk, steady, steel, stern, strained, strapped, straps, stretching, strong, struggled, struggling, stuffed, stung, subjugate, submissively, submit, sullied, suppressed, surging, surrender, sustained, taboo, taking her, taunting, thrashing, tied, tightly, tingling, tore, torturously, trapped, twat, undulations, unrelenting, unwilling, violent, volition, vulnerable, wailing, weeping, whimper, whip, wild, will, willpower, withholding, withdraw, witnessed, wound tightly, wrapped, wrists, yank, yielded

Thank You from

Choose A Sexy Ending Erotic Books

More

Cover Art and Illustrations

The beautiful clear, crisp vector art on our cover is by
Sophie B. Olsen, a very talented artist and author. Her work is also
featured in The Princess and the Pirate, the illustrations dotting our
text. You can learn more at Sophie's website:
www.sophiebolsen.com.

Coming Soon from CASE ebooks

Texas Trio

by Stefanie Olsen

When Catherine Connor's domineering aunt dies, her
formerly meek uncle shows his true colors. Cat is desperate to save
her sister and their beloved Nanny, but is she desperate enough to
depend on a thief?

An arranged marriage with a wealthy Argentinian
landowner seems like a better choice than the blue-eyed burglar, but
Uncle Harry's not the only one with secrets. Cat's discovering maybe
she's not the person she thought she was, either, because no well-
bred young lady dreams about doing the things dancing through her
mind these days.

It's 1880 and the Gulf Coast of Texas has never been this
steamy. Stefanie Olsen's Texas Trio series is just getting started, and
you won't want to miss out on all this fun!

Printed in Great Britain
by Amazon.co.uk, Ltd.,
Marston Gate.